In Search of

RELIGIOUS

MATURITY

In Search of
RELIGIOUS
MATURITY

ALEXANDER FEINSILVER

THE ANTIOCH PRESS   •   1960

Published by The Antioch Press
Yellow Springs, Ohio

Printed in the United States of America

To Lillian

CONTENTS

PERSON TO PERSON

This book was written for two reasons. First, I felt such a book ought to be written; second, I thought I was the one to write it. Perhaps these two reasons lie behind the writing of every book; they probably should. In any case, these were my reasons, and I would like to explain them.

I felt such a book should be written because so much else has already been written along these lines. That may seem strange, for one would not ordinarily feel the need for additional writing in a field in which a good deal has already been said. Yet I felt that much of what has recently been written about the art of living and the relevance of religion to it has not struck the note of challenge. It has, in large measure, sought to be reassuring and has often avoided the direct confrontation of some basic issues of life and faith. Its psychology and theology may have been helpful to many but have not always been such as to appeal to the more mature reader.

We are living in a period of considerable tension. This has created a widespread mood of anxiety. The insights of psychology and religion have been rightly recognized as sources of stability and direction for the perplexed of our day. In the quest for values that is characteristic of our

time, attempts have been made to distill the essence of these
two disciplines, to bring them into harmony, to apply them
to the problems of individual living and personal faith. But
not always maturely enough.

If our new-found faith is to be genuine and meaningful;
if it is to be suited to the needs of men and women of the
mid-twentieth century; if it is to contribute anything at all
to the development of values for our day and for the building
of a better tomorrow, it must be a challenging and mature
faith. Such a faith would not only help men find their place
in the scheme of things but raise them to a new sense of their
own dignity, their own responsibility toward the molding
of their lives and the future of the race. If we prize maturity
in the mental and emotional sphere, we must cherish it in
the religious realm as well. That is the substance of this book.
And because little or nothing has been written about formulating a mature faith, I thought it ought to be done.

But why should *I* write it? One answer might be that
since someone ought to do it, it might as well be myself.
But it seems to me that my particular personal history and
professional experience predisposed me to it. My under-
graduate training, unlike that of most men in the ministry,
was in the sciences. This early training in scientific method,
and the temper of the twenties during which it was received,
instilled in me a high regard for the laboratory and test tube
as avenues for the discovery of truth, an appreciation for the
method of experiment and the meaning of evidence. My
ministry—now covering over two decades—has also some
element of uniqueness. Half of it has been devoted to work
with university students, half to congregational activity. Thus
I may be able to view the need for religious maturity from
the standpoints of both young people and adults seeking to
find a meaningful basis for faith. It is my hope that this
presentation may help clarify some of the fundamental issues
which must be grappled with in that process and that it may

thereby serve in some measure to channel the current interest in religion into avenues of greater personal growth.

Some of this material was used in a series of talks given over the Purdue University radio station while I ministered to the Jewish students on that campus. I am grateful for the response accorded to those talks and hope that the present enlargement on the themes discussed may be similarly received by a wider audience.

—A. F.

In Search of

RELIGIOUS

MATURITY

1

GROWING UP RELIGIOUSLY

Are You Religious?

According to a poll conducted by the *Catholic Digest,* ninety-nine per cent of the American people profess a belief in God. Of these, eighty-seven per cent feel "absolutely certain" of the existence of God, ten per cent are "fairly sure," and two per cent are "not quite sure," though not doubtful enough to classify themselves as unbelievers.

Offhand, these figures may seem comforting to the religionist. However, the statement that ninety-nine per cent of our people "believe in God" is a quantitative, not qualitative, measure. It may indicate how many people accept the idea of God, but tells us nothing about the *character* of that belief.

Just what do those in the ninety-nine per cent group mean when they say they believe in God? And just what do those in the one per cent category mean when they say they do not believe in God? And, probing into the motivations *behind* belief and unbelief, why do the ninety-nine per cent believe, and why do the one per cent not believe, in God?

Turning first to the one per cent, I would expect them to be a group diversified in their habits and outlook. It is equally likely that the God they say they don't believe in varies considerably, and that their reasons for not believing also vary. In some cases, the rebellion against the belief in

God may be the rebellion against a childish conception of God as a big man with a white beard. In other cases, it may be a rebellion against any form of belief in God—as a reaction against the father image, if the father of that individual has been unduly harsh or severe.

A student once said to me, "Anyone who believes in God ought to have his head examined." To which I replied, "I see. But don't you think anyone who rejects the idea of God also ought to have his head examined?" He turned upon me and asked, "Why? What do you mean?" "First," I replied, "I'll tell you what *you* mean. You mean that anyone who believes in God is projecting the father image, right?" When he assented, I continued, "Well, if *projecting* the father image means that one needs the attention of a psychiatrist, *rejection* of God, or the father image, would require psychiatric attention as well. Surely rejection of the father image indicates a much more serious problem."

In most cases, there is also likely to be a semantic problem—a problem of words and meanings—involved in the rejection of God, for different people mean different things when they use the term "God." It is even possible that one who says he does *not* believe in God may hold the same views as one who says he *does*. The individual who says he does *not* believe in God may simply refuse to believe in a God who possesses human attributes. He may be rejecting the anthropomorphisms of the Bible, since it is from the Bible that he absorbed his earliest notions of God. He may be unwilling to believe that the "voice of God" actually was heard, that the "hand of the Lord" really acted. But the individual who says he believes in God may not take these Biblical phrases in a literal sense at all. He may reject the literal acceptance of these terms, yet not reject the idea of God in some more profound sense. Thus believer and unbeliever may be in greater agreement than either of them will admit—or even recognize.

In the case of the ninety-nine per cent who say they do believe in God, just as in the case of those who say they do not believe, we could also raise the question, Why? Some may believe in God because their parents have been church members, because they have been recipients of religious education and are convinced by their training that God exists. Others may be even more deeply committed to a belief in God by some personal experience of great moment in their lives. Still others—and perhaps the majority—of those who profess to believe may simply accept the belief because almost everyone else does, because it is the expected thing.

One might legitimately ask, Just what does that belief mean so far as the believers' daily living is concerned? For example, the simple question might be raised, Do all of these people go to the church or synagogue regularly? As the poll itself indicates, this is far from true. Only sixty-two per cent of the Catholics, twenty-five per cent of the Protestants, and twelve per cent of the Jews attend services every week. And we find a number of Catholics, Protestants, and Jews who say they believe in God yet *never* go to the church or synagogue.

Further, one might ask of those who attend services regularly, to what extent is their attendance a truly religious force in their lives? Do they put their religion into practice through ethical living, or is the process for them a weekly "emotional massage"? And it might be worth discovering how many of those who do not attend services, and how many of those who attend irregularly, have a genuinely spiritual outlook and pattern of living. Haven't we all known non-attending believers, and even so-called atheists, who lived more religiously than some "pillars" of the church or synagogue?

It would seem important to ask the ninety-nine per cent who profess a belief in God just what *kind* of God they believe in. Although more varieties are possible, we might submit three different concepts of God to them, and ask them to check the one closest to their own.

The first might be this: *Do you believe in a single, cosmic force at work in this universe, underlying all of life and all of the manifestations of nature?* This is probably as liberal an approach to the idea of God as we can get. Yet the question makes no reference to an intelligent force, or a moral force, or supernatural force, and the person answering this question in the affirmative and regarding himself as a believer in God might not be accepted as such by many a good churchman.

A second choice might be: *Do you believe in an intelligent, moral force at work in this universe?* That would narrow the question considerably. A person answering this question affirmatively would be embraced by most religionists, since intelligence and morality are generally regarded as the key attributes of divinity. Yet if we narrowed the question still further, we would run into trouble.

Suppose we asked, as a third alternative, *Do you believe in a personal God, interested in your individual welfare?* Probably a great many of those who profess to believe in God would not go so far as to accept this definition of God; yet from the standpoint of traditional religion, in both the church and synagogue, God is interested in the individual, God is personal, as well as an intelligent and moral being.

Students and adults have sometimes asked me, "What is *your* definition of 'God'?"—without even bothering to sit down for an answer. To this I have generally replied, "How much time do you have?" This may seem evasive, and generally evokes a puzzled look. But the fact is that those who raise the question seek an easy answer, and I find it necessary to explain that I would like to explore the question with them, so that *they* might find an answer, adding that any definition that I provide would represent the result of *my* thinking, not theirs, and might not meet *their* needs or match *their* maturity, so that it could not be too meaningful for them. I would like the reader, as well, to reach his own definition. If my use of the term seems to include all three of the above concepts, I hope that the later discussion will justify that usage.

How many people have even thought about these matters? Most people carry infantile notions of God; the concept of God has not grown with them, as they have grown, but has been arrested in its development at the adolescent level. And is it not strange that we should be satisfied with adolescent or pre-adolescent conceptions of God when we are not satisfied with adolescent or pre-adolescent conceptions of art, science, or music? Why can't we grow in our understanding of religion just as we grow in our understanding of other aspects of life?

In our religious development, it is as if we stopped with simple arithmetic, instead of going on to algebra and geometry, in mathematics; or as if we stopped with the march or waltz, instead of going on to the concerto or symphony, in the realm of music. Yet it is even more important to mature religiously than it is to mature in our understanding of mathematics or music. While a greater understanding of mathematics or music may be desirable, this does not so directly affect our lives as what we believe about the universe we live in, about the relationship of man to the universe and of man to man. What we believe can and should make a difference in how we live, in our relationship with others. It can and should make a difference in how we live with ourselves as well.

I have no argument with the man of simple faith. I have known such men and women, individuals who are good and noble, at peace with the world and at peace with themselves. Yet for many today, exposed to an inquiring approach, living in a world of experimentation and analysis, faith must be fortified by reason. For many of us moderns, the challenge is not for a *return to* religion, if by a return to religion is meant simple surrender to the doctrines of church and synagogue, but an *advance in* religion, an advance in our own religious thinking.

There are probably more people now who believe in God than there were in the third decade of this century, the turbulent twenties. Today, belief in God is more fashionable than it was then. But is that good? Not if by this return to religion we mean a retreat from reason, a weariness of the mind, a willingness to "let God do it" when we stand at an impasse in our own lives or in the life of society.

We need religion today; we need faith in God. But our faith must be able to stand up under scrutiny; it must be able to weather the storms of doubt and despair; it must be able to stimulate and challenge us to nobler living; it must be able to transform us, and through us, the life of mankind.

What Is Mature Religion?

We have been considerably exposed in recent years to the concept of maturity. We no longer think of maturity as the time when one reaches the age of twenty-one and is allowed to vote. We have heard of emotional maturity and of the mature mind, and are by now aware that chronological maturity does not guarantee either of these.

Neither does it guarantee religious maturity. Maturity implies growth, whether it be in the realm of the mind, in the area of the emotions, or on the biological level. And one can grow or fail to grow religiously, as one can grow or fail to grow in other ways. What is more, we can grow in one aspect of our personality without experiencing equal growth in others. A college professor, presumably possessing a mature mind, may yet harbor racial or religious prejudice, thereby revealing emotional immaturity, the haunting presence of insecurity and fear. So we find men and women who, regardless of the degree of maturity they have reached in other aspects of their growth, display in their religious thinking fears and dependencies, or hostilities and aggressions, which mark them as religiously immature.

There are those who regard religion, like sex—and perhaps politics—as something you just don't discuss. It is a kind of private domain, an area of our personal lives in which each of us must find his own way. I am, of course, aware of the democratic right of private judgment in the matter of religion and am all for it. But how is one to achieve sexual maturity, political maturity, or religious maturity, unless these matters are discussed? And how can religion be rendered at all effective in our lives if, in the zeal to protect our religious privacy, we conceal our convictions not only from the prying eyes of others, but from our own intelligent scrutiny? An individual grows, not by secluding himself on a desert island, but by associating with people. Ideas grow in the same way, not by being locked up, but by contact with other ideas, through reading and conversation.

There are, of course, those who refuse to discuss religion, not because it is a private affair, but because, from their point of view, it simply isn't worth talking about. These are the "emancipated" individuals, who feel, as the German expresses it, *"Es ist alles Humbug wo die Glocke klingt"*: "All is humbug where the church-bell rings." But they ignore the fact that religion, through the ages, has been a seed-bed of inspiration for art, literature, and music; that mankind seems somehow incurably religious; that religion can still be a potent force in the life of the individual and in civilization; and that this force, freed from the shackles of fear and superstition, can be rendered magnificently creative for the individual and society.

Protestations of the "enlightened" that religion isn't important run counter to the fact that there is in our land today a new interest in religion. If this means nothing to them, it is certainly important as one of the most amazing social phenomena of the mid-twentieth century. A generation ago, religion seemed to be on its way out; today it appears to be on its way back. Some of the best-selling books in the non-fiction field in recent years have been religious books. More money is being contributed to churches and synagogues today than ever before, and this is not merely due to inflation, for church membership and construction have also increased. Individuals as far apart as movie stars and atomic scientists are joining these churches. And Hollywood has capitalized on this new interest in religion with a whole series of religious films.

These days we are being reminded to attend worship services by newspaper ads, bus and subway cards, and even automobile stickers. Indeed, I cannot pour a drink of milk from its container without being reminded, in bold-face type, to "Take your family to church on Sunday." (Our milk supplier doubtless forgot that some of his customers worship on a different Sabbath, or he might have broadened the wording!) And on a recent trip on which I had occasion to travel by bus, I ate at the station restaurant and found place-mats on the tables containing the text of Catholic, Protestant, and Jewish versions of grace before meals.

What is perhaps more significant is the increasing recognition given to God by our government. We have placed God recently in the pledge of allegiance to our flag, which means that no conscientious non-believer can now repeat that pledge; the mail we receive carries the cancellation "Pray for Peace"; and the phrase "In God We Trust," long used on our coins, is now being printed on our bank-notes as well. When this was suggested to Lincoln, he jestingly offered as an alternate proposal, "Silver and gold have I none, but such as I have I give unto thee."

In this period of international insecurity and personal

tension, men are once again seeking faith. But the type of
faith now being generated may not be what we want or need.
It may not contribute to our religious maturity but may simply
be an expression of our religious immaturity. It may be a
new type of "fire insurance," insuring us not against the fire
and brimstone of a theological hell, but against the raging
conflagration of atomic war. It may be emergency religion
or "foxhole religion," as it was known to the men in the
Second World War, and may spend itself once the crisis
is past.

If that "crisis" should stay with us, this newly popular
faith may take on more and more the character of an escape
from reality. It may become a flight from confrontation, a
closing of the eyes, a stopping of the ears, a shutting of the
mind, to the demands that are made upon us by the world
we live in, because we are too weak or cowardly to face those
demands and meet them squarely. Religion may become a
hiding-place from life. And this we should want to avoid.

On the other hand, this new interest in religion may
carry within it the prospect of new progress in our spiritual
development. Religious thinking can become a compelling
and invigorating influence in our lives. We live in a time when
the best thought and noblest ideals must be harnessed together
for the making of a better world, or at least for the saving
of this one, and in that task religion can play a distinctive
role: its historical and ideological potential are tremendous.

But mature religion, the attempt to relate man to himself
and to the world about him on an adult level, cannot be
achieved by immature people. The immature are not prepared
for the synthesis of all of life's fears and frustrations, its
hopes and dreams, its personal and social involvements, its
infinite potentialities and infinite challenge, which mature
religion represents. In the absence of the mature mind, and
of emotional maturity, some religious synthesis may be made

—indeed, it is likely to be made. But it will carry with it the logical weaknesses, the childish dependencies, and the ultimate inadequacy so closely associated with immaturity of any kind.

We are today experiencing that great hunger of which the prophet spoke, which is not a hunger for bread, but for the living word of God. Our generation must not attempt to satisfy that spiritual hunger through retreat to the religious formulations of a pre-scientific age; it must attempt to satisfy its spiritual needs through advance, through growth in religious comprehension. The language of faith must somehow be couched in the accents of the atomic age.

But between retreat and advance, and basic to determining the direction we are to take, lie rediscovery and reassessment. Beneath the encrustations of history and habit lie the treasures of true spirituality, of fruitful and fulfilling faith. We must do some exploring to discover them.

A Note of Caution

At the present state of religious awareness in our nation, some words of caution are perhaps in order. For there are several dangers involved in the popularizing of religion through the mass media. There is the possibility of making a "fad" of religion, and there are the dangers of sentimentalism, obscurantism, and opportunism. Suppose we look at each of these for a moment.

Faddism is a familiar feature of American life and could even befall religion. We have had fads in foods, clothing, hair styles, dances, slang, and music. Some of us are old enough to remember the fourteen-day diet, the low-waisted dress that ended just above the knee, "bangs," the Charleston (in its first invasion), "Oh, you kid!," and "Yes, We Have No Bananas." Occasionally, the fads of yesterday are revived, but ordinarily they are displaced by new fads.

It is a well-known fact that no two objects can occupy the same space at the same time, and by the same token new fads crowd out old ones. There is something obviously "dated" about the fourteen-day diet, the flapper's dress, "bangs," the Charleston, "Oh, you kid!," and "Yes, We Have No Bananas." And if we revert to any of these from time to time, it is with considerably less enthusiasm and wholeheartedness than attended their original onrush.

Because of the peculiar power of mass communication and the universal drive toward imitation, fads are easily started. Witness the Davy Crockett craze, which just a short time ago was so rampant in song and attire. No American child was happy without some Davy Crockett item in his wardrobe, and even Polly Crockett hats had to be produced to satisfy all the little sisters that yearned to "get into the act." Today, none of these young frontiersmen or their sisters would be caught wearing or using what yesterday they so proudly displayed. Just as surely as Davy Crockett supplanted Hopalong Cassidy, so in turn was he displaced by Zorro.

The same power of mass communication and drive toward imitation can stimulate a new interest in religion, and seems, indeed, to have done so. But how lasting will be its effect, how real will be its impact? Is it not at least possible that the present interest in "religion" may be just another fad? For magazines, radio, and television, always on the lookout for new gambits to reach the public, "religion" can supply welcome new material. They may use it for all it is worth, to the point of saturation, then drop it, and the religious "jag" may soon wear off. The "return to religion" may be followed by a "return to normalcy," to making money and having fun. A decade from now some of today's "religious" magazine articles, popular songs, and programs on radio and TV may seem as dated as "Barney Google." Those who are genuinely concerned about religion would not want this to happen. They should be the first to warn that it may.

The second danger in the present situation is the danger of religiosity. That is, religion may degenerate into banality, in the same way that sentiment may deteriorate into sentimentalism. Just as sentimentalism is obvious, superficial, and a caricature of true sentiment, so can religiosity be obvious, superficial, and a caricature of religion. The possibility of sentimentalism is a real one, as can be seen every Mother's Day. It is, of course, proper to love one's mother and even to make some gesture from time to time to reveal one's affection for her. But an institution like Mother's Day can easily be surrounded by songs and slogans which convert honest senti-ment into sentimentalism—to say nothing of the commercial-ism that converts the sentiment into cash.

Religion becomes religiosity when, as in the case of sentiment and sentimentalism, the outward expression is more important than the inner feeling. Both religion and sentiment ought to be more than skin deep, more than a sweet-smelling bubble bath in which we submerge ourselves periodically—or lounge continuously—to "smell sweet." Where there are flowers, there will be fragrance; where there is genuine relig-ious feeling, there will be goodness and love. Nor does one cultivate flowers by wearing them on the lapel but by water-ing their roots and removing the weeds, working at the level of the soil as well as below it, to produce the beauty and frag-rance of the flower. Cultivating religion, one must similarly nurture the roots and pull out the weeds if religion is to blos-som properly in the life of the individual. It must have depth to have vitality; it must be firmly grounded if it is to flower.

A third danger is the danger of obscurantism or mys-ticism. That is, the religious mood may be cloudy rather than clear, a kind of haze or aura which surrounds us, as the amniotic sac protects the infant in the womb. The unborn child is warm, is fed, is protected from the stresses and strains of the outside world for which it is not yet ready. It is alive; yet its life is rather attenuated. Protected against contact with the world outside, it is unable to see the grass or hear the birds. Its senses are as yet unawakened; they can only be awakened through a confrontation of the world, not in hiding from it. Nature has so planned it that the unborn child prefers the light of day, with all its hopes and all its hazards, to the soft, warm darkness, and so emerges to meet life literally "head-on."

If we are to be maturely religious, we must be no less daring than the infant. We ought not to be satisfied to cloister ourselves in a creed or use the church as an escape from challenge. Church and creed we may have—indeed, we ought to have—but rather as expressions of our facing up to life. These should provide us with aims and purposes; they must not themselves become our objectives. The navel cord that supplies nutrition to the unborn child can also destroy the child by strangulation. This must not be allowed to happen, either to the child's source of nutrition or to the sources of religious inspiration. Mature religion is characterized by courage and conviction, not by cowardice and confusion. Mature religion, like the new-born child, meets life's challenge head-on.

The final danger to religion is the danger of opportunism. That is, the attempt to make of religion an instrument for success, happiness, and social acceptance. One might find that a religious approach to one's employer, employees, or customers pays dividends in terms of cash earnings. That is far from impossible, in spite of a widespread notion that you can't mix religion with business. Yet the possibility that common decency may actually prove profitable should not be the motivation behind religious thought or conduct. This is as objectionable as the statement, "Honesty is the best policy." For even if honesty were the *worst* policy, we ought to be honest; and even if religion *"doesn't"* pay" we ought to be religious, to achieve a sound religious philosophy of life.

Religion can be grossly distorted by the attitude of

"What's in it for me?" Religion is more than merely a useful device for attaining poise or business success. It is a way of looking at the universe and the phenomenon of life, at other human beings, and at one's own self. It is a program for living based upon that over-all view of life. The opportunist approach to religion would put religion in the category of certain soaps, toothpastes, and deodorants which advertise their power to make you popular and prevent you from being a wall-flower. While it is true that religion can give one serenity and poise, these are derived, if they are genuine and lasting, from "seeing life whole," with its limitations as well as its potentialities, its disillusionments and frustrations as well as its hopes and aspirations, its pain as well as its promise. Any religion which presents only the promise of life, without heed to its pain, is certainly superficial. Mature religion is as different from that as a diamond brooch is different from a piece of costume jewelry.

Criteria for Maturity

How are we to distinguish between mature and immature religion? Some of the material presented in the press, on the radio and television, is of higher calibre than others; but some of it may be described as nothing more than "religious soap-opera." While one does not like to speak disparagingly of religious programming, one ought to recognize that even religious material can run the gamut from excellence of conception and presentation to travesty and distortion.

After all, religion is in the process of being "rediscovered." As material for mass media it is, in a sense, new. Those responsible for interpreting it must discover not only proper techniques for its presentation but, what is even more important, just what it is they are trying to say. While the techniques of presentation may follow those already developed successfully in selling household articles, the message must not be lost sight of. The techniques may be acceptable, even excellent, yet the message may not be worthy of the method. Conversely, and this may be more the pity, the message may be a sound one, yet the method of presentation inadequate, amateurish, or even fatuous.

How much agreement is there on what religion is, or ought to be? Centuries ago, long before the opening of the Christian era, my ancestors worshipped God in the Temple at Jerusalem by offering sacrifices to Him at the altar. Small or large animals were presented for the holocaust, depending on the wealth of the individual or the degree of sin for which he was atoning. Today Jews would be inclined to say—as indeed the prophets proclaimed even in those days—that this type of religious expression does not truly represent Judaism at its highest. But just what is Judaism? Ask any two Jews, and you will find that you get two different answers.

Is there any greater agreement among Christians as to what constitutes Christianity? Some months ago the papers reported a large sum of money bequeathed to "worthy Christians." A great deal of discussion took place as to just what was meant by a Christian. I do not recall how the case ended, but it is interesting that a civil judge, to whom the adjudication of the case was entrusted, was charged with the responsibility of defining a Christian. Needless to say, the various definitions provided by many well-meaning people from numerous church groups did not serve to make his decision easier.

Within the American scene, more than in any country on earth, religion takes many forms. A minister in the deep South recently was bitten by a snake which he had been handling to prove that faith was more powerful than the snake. After he was bitten, and began showing evidence of being ill, he was asked to take medical treatment but refused, as this might impugn the strength of his faith. He died of that snakebite—and the coroner called it suicide, as indeed it was.

In another recent incident, a man in pursuit of his

religion whipped his wife and another woman to death. His religion taught that all were sinners, and that they must whip one another in expiation of their sins. But the women died, and he was hailed into court for murder, even though freedom of religious expression is guaranteed by our Constitution. I am sure that no reader will feel that the practice of religion ought to be tolerated even if it includes murder. The judge in the case did not.

What, then, is religion? Perhaps the poorest place to find a definition of religion would be the dictionary, but let us see what it says. There we find not one definition of religion, but many, with illustrations and quotations to boot. Apparently the compilers of the dictionary were so overwhelmed by the task of defining the term that they offer us a variety of meanings. Left with the power of choice, I would choose two. One is from the Old Testament, the other is from the New. The first is from Micah: "To do justice, to love mercy, and to walk humbly with thy God." The second is from James: "To visit the fatherless and widows in their affliction and to keep oneself unspotted from the world."

Notice that these sublime expressions of the human spirit, Jewish and Christian alike, make no mention of ritual. Ritual may be important and even necessary as a medium of religious expression, but the essence of religion, as expressed by Micah and James, lies in two things: personal purity and social conscience. Live decently and love others is the substance of their teachings. Religion, from their point of view, is more than a preoccupation with theological concepts. It is a *modus vivendi,* a way of life. In our time, it might be best exemplified by Gandhi in his teaching of non-violence, and by Albert Schweitzer in his principle of reverence for life.

But you may ask, "Aren't you just equating religion with goodness? And isn't religion really something more than that?" My answer would be that I am not merely equating religion with goodness—though we could find many worse things to equate it with—and religion really *is* something more than that.

While the teachings of Micah and James, Gandhi and Schweitzer, are seemingly non-theological, theirs is in every instance a religious philosophy, based on foundations of religious belief. What we most deeply believe serves to mold our approach to life and to determine our daily acts of living. These men have believed—and we, as religious men and women, can believe—that there is order in this universe and on our planet; that life is no mere accident and man is something more than just another animal; that he has dignity and divinity within him. Because they believed these things, they sought to extend the symmetry found in nature into an orderly arrangement of human relations and to translate the dignity and divinity in man into the decency of men. And these remain the chief aims of religion today.

What, then, are the criteria by which we are to distinguish mature from immature religious faith? They can be expressed in three R's: the test of Reason, of Responsibility, and of Relatedness.

Religion which does not meet the test of reason can be distorted into faddism, sentimentalism, obscurantism, or opportunism, previously discussed. It may be temporary and evanescent, it may be inane and insincere, it may be fuzzy and escapist, it may be practical and useful, but it is not mature. For mature religion is full-grown, well-rooted, sturdy, and strong. It has faced reality and met challenge. It has come to terms with psychology and sociology, geology and archaeology. These disciplines of the mind have poured their sunlight upon it, watered its roots, nurtured its shoots, beautified its flowering. Religion tested by reason does not easily wither, is not easily uprooted, does not quickly die. It has become an essential part of the individual, operating in harmony with all that he knows and sees, and integrating all of the experiences of life into one comprehensible pattern.

The second test of mature religion is the test of responsibility. If religion is geared only to the needs or desires of the individual, without regard to his duties—to his responsibilities —it is not mature religion. Faddism, sentimentalism, obscurantism, or opportunism place little emphasis on the prophetic note in religion, on its deepest ethical convictions, on its compelling moral character. Responsible religion directs our attention not only inward to a preoccupation with our own needs and desires, but outward, to a recognition of our duties and responsibilities to others. Mature religion serves not merely "to comfort the afflicted," but also to "afflict the comfortable." The maturely religious man will be interested in civil liberties and in the conquest of illiteracy, poverty, disease, and war. The validity, the vitality, the very value of his religion will be tested in the way his faith sensitizes him to the problems of life, fortifies him for surmounting them.

Finally, there is the test of relatedness. If a man's religious faith is displayed in his sense of responsibility, it is because that sense of responsibility is engendered by a sense of relatedness. What is it that makes us *feel* responsible for others? What moves us to consider the needs of others, to do things for others? It is the conviction that we and other human beings are part of some larger design and that we and they have some importance in that design; that the importance of others is as great as our own, that what happens to them is somehow happening to us. Mature religion serves to relate us to the physical universe and to our fellowmen—with all the knowledge at our disposal, and with all the love we can command.

The Dilemma Before Us

It has been said that in this Age of Anxiety there are only two kinds of people: those who admit their anxiety, and those who attempt to conceal it. This widespread anxiety may be due in part to the fact that we live in troubled times of international suspicion and misunderstanding, of changing social and economic patterns, which make it difficult to feel secure and at home in this world.

Yet our anxiety is due not so much to these environmental factors as to our inner environment—the attitudes with which we face these external facts. I have known men who could take a great deal of pressure and frustration yet come up from beneath it all, ready to go on. And I have met those who, under the slightest pressures, have "folded up" and stopped trying. The equilibrium of a pair of scales is affected not only by the balance of the weights placed upon it, but also by the firmness of the fulcrum of support which serves to hold the weight. And much the same thing is true on the human level. If anxiety and neurosis are prevalent today, we might well question the firmness of our "fulcrum."

Some time ago, a boy at Yale committed suicide. He left a note saying that he saw no reason in life, therefore saw no reason for continuing to live. And more recently, you may have read about a young man, twenty-three years of age, wealthy, married, and the father of a child, who took an airplane aloft, circled about until he ran out of gas, then plunged to earth, crashing his plane and killing himself. Why should he have done so? We cannot, of course, know all of the external circumstances or the psychological, and perhaps subconscious, motivations that led him to his death. But it is safe to say that, whatever these may have been, the real conditions which caused his death lay not outside himself but within himself—not in the condition *of* life but in his attitude *toward* life.

If today more than ever men tend to feel insecure and anxiety-ridden, it is not merely because of the threat of atomic war, real as that may be. Nor is it altogether due to the complexities of life in our day, with our big city stresses, our economic pressures, our machinery-ridden homes and offices, which may prompt us to seek out a quiet island in the South Pacific. There is something much deeper that disturbs men. It is something of the feeling of the Yale student who killed himself. It is something of the feeling of the young man who crashed to death in his plane. It is the gnawing suspicion that life just makes no sense, that life simply has no purpose or meaning. That feeling makes a mockery of all our joys, a sham of all our efforts, a veritable nightmare of all our disappointments and frustrations.

Yet here is the dilemma in which many find themselves. They have no inner source of strength and are tied to nothing strong outside themselves. They have no spiritual moorings. They are cast about like driftwood on the sea of life, tossed about by the waves and storms, the rebuffs which beset them. They lack proper anchorage *in* life; they lack faith in the very meaning *of* life.

The spiritual moorings which serve to give us stability, to give us anchorage, are the forces of love and faith. It is through these that we give support to our lives, for it is through these that we attach ourselves to someone or something beyond ourselves. Without that attachment we are alone and likely to feel weak. That attachment gives us strength, just as surely as the attachment of a log in the river to another log or to the river bank gives it the power to resist the current of the stream.

Many have found purpose in life through their love for their families. The family rescues us from self-absorption and serves as a wider orbit of interest. The sense of responsibility for it, the pleasures derived from it, and above all the sense of solidarity with it, are stabilizing influences. It has even been found that group attachments (an extension of the family) play some part in preventing personality breakdown.

A fortunate few have also found meaning in life through their love for their work. You may remember the conversation between Grand and Dr. Rieux in the novel *The Plague* by

Albert Camus. An epidemic of Bubonic plague has broken out in the city of Oran. The people of the community are bewildered, to the point of panic. The doctor inquires of Grand how he is facing the situation, and Grand, the writer, replies, "After all, I've my work."

That linkage to others, in which, paradoxically, we submerge ourselves only to realize ourselves the more fully, or that devotion to a life-work peculiarly suited to our talents and most highly expressing our true nature, have often served to give men a degree of anchorage and stability.

But there remains the matter of faith, the feeling that life itself has meaning, that it "makes sense." The young man who crashed to death in his plane had a family, and presumably loved them. Yet that love was not strong enough to provide him with a purpose in living. Perhaps if he were an artist or musician and felt constrained to live for his art or his music, he might have wanted to live. But if his love for his family could not keep him from suicide, even his devotion to his chosen task might not have been able to do so. What was missing was faith.

But therein lies the difficulty; to a great many in our day, faith seems no longer possible. Faith in what? Ours is a generation that has advanced beyond the orthodoxies and certainties of an earlier day, yet has found no substitute source of strength, no substitute faith.

We are heirs of Copernicus and know that the earth is not the center of creation. This has led us to question our world's centrality in the universal scheme of things. We have generally accepted Darwinism and are ready to concede that man is related to the rest of the animal world. This has led us to question man's uniqueness. We have been influenced by Freud and recognize that much of human behavior is subconsciously motivated. This has impugned our capacity as creatures of free moral choice.

Copernicus, Darwin, and Freud cast their shadows over

any attempt to achieve a mature religious synthesis. We cannot dismiss them. We can no longer dogmatize about religion but must instead rethink some basic issues. What is man? How free are we? Is God possible? Is death the end? These are some of the fundamental questions that must be raised anew. These questions are not easily answered. But it is only through an honest effort to do so that we can dispel the doubts that beset us and approach a solution to our dilemma. It is only through such an effort that we can achieve a measure of inner integration, a mature religious faith.

2

FACING BASIC ISSUES

What Is Man?

Just what is man? How important a creature is he?

Every now and then, we read of the discovery of stars of tremendous size, hundreds of light years distant from the earth. These new insights into a larger universe have greatly affected our thinking about man's place in the cosmic scheme. Now that we no longer think of the earth as the center of the universe and no longer think of man as the product of a special act of creation, we may be inclined to regard man as a creature of relatively small significance with perhaps an exaggerated sense of his own importance.

But does our expanded knowledge of a larger and more intricate universe really reduce man's stature? Some time ago, a conversation was reported between an astronomer and a layman. The astronomer remarked, "As I scan the heavens with a telescope, I am struck with the thought that man is, after all, a creature of small account." But to this the layman replied, "Aren't you forgetting that man is the astronomer who has discovered the immensity of the universe? Aren't you forgetting that it is man who invented the very telescope which you use?"

The universe is indeed vast and complex; yet it is man who has discovered this fact. And man, who has been able to build telescopes to survey the heavens, can hardly be called an insignificant creature. His is the seeing eye, the inquiring mind, the comprehending brain. He is the great explorer of the universe in which he lives. Nothing is too big or too small for him. The immensities of interstellar space and the intricacies of the atom become the subject of his investigation.

There are those who turn to the biological sciences to demonstrate that man is a creature of lowly origin, not too different from the beasts. We have indeed discovered that it is not man alone who has a brain but that his brain is merely more highly developed than that of the other animals. The dog has more intelligence than the earthworm because his brain, the central part of his nervous system, is more complex than that of the earthworm. And man has more intelligence than the dog, simply because his brain possesses more convolutions. There is no essential difference, we are sometimes told, between man and the lower animals; the difference is simply one of degree, not of kind. Man therefore has no right to regard himself as a creature totally different from the rest, as a being who is somehow unique.

That is, of course, partly true. However, there is so great a gap between man and the rest of animal life as to constitute almost an essential difference between them. Given the steel and cement necessary for the construction of a bridge, no other creature could produce the structure which spans the Hudson River in New York or the Golden Gate in California. No other creature has thus far been able to compose a poem comparable to Keats's "Endymion" or anything that sounds like Beethoven's Ninth Symphony.

It can be demonstrated from the field of chemistry that there is no unique element in man's physical makeup which sets him off as distinct from the rest of creation. Chemically speaking, we are told, the human body contains enough iron to produce a two-penny nail, enough carbon to produce a dozen lead pencils, enough water to fill a four-gallon jug.

Man consists largely of carbon, oxygen, hydrogen, and nitrogen, in fixed proportions.

Yet this combination of carbon, oxygen, hydrogen, and nitrogen has been able to fly over continents, to tunnel through mountains and under water. This same man has been able to take the tissue of a human eye and transplant it onto the eye of another, restoring the power of sight. He has been able to draw blood from one human body to save the life of another. Is he really a helpless, totally dependent creature?

Hardly. Man is a creature of unparalleled mental power, capable of producing a Newton, a Galileo, an Einstein. He is a creature of unparalleled imaginative power, boasting of a Shakespeare and a Leonardo da Vinci. Above all, man is a creature of tremendous spiritual capabilities, able to produce an Isaiah, a Confucius, a Jesus. Every discovery which man makes, every poem he writes, every church he builds must serve to impress us with man's greatness; every achievement must be further indication to us that, far from being an insignificant creature, he is rather a creature with unusual endowments and fascinating potentialities.

What, then, can we expect from man? The current answer among some religionists is: not much. Hasn't man invented the atomic and hydrogen bombs, weapons of tremendous destructiveness? What hope is there that he will be able to keep these weapons from destroying himself? The tendency is to denigrate man, to belittle man in the process of exalting God. Mature religion holds a higher estimate of man. It trusts man, as it trusts God.

If man is to solve the many problems that confront him in today's world, his courage and confidence must be bolstered, not broken. The individual is, in some measure, what he thinks he is, what he is told he is. If a person holds a low estimate of himself, if he is constantly reminded of his limitations, he is not likely to achieve much or even attempt much.

Man's morale can be shattered and his initiative crushed by
the mental picture he holds of himself as a creature of small
account.

There is the danger, amidst the complexities of today's
world, that men individually and mankind collectively may
experience what has been called a "failure of nerve." There
are times when each of us feels that the pressures of life are
too much for us, the challenges too great. Such a mood, if
extended through our modern world, can be calamitous,
paralyzing all constructive and creative effort.

Surely man should have faith in God; it can mean much
to him in seeking out the directions in which he is to use his
energies. But he must also have faith in himself if he is to use
these energies at all. If we display no faith in man, we display
little faith in God, for man is God's chief handiwork. While
man's limitations are real and should be recognized, his
potentialities are great and should not be minimized. For
man is largely responsible for the difficulties of our day, and
it is mainly through his conscious efforts that these problems
can be transcended. Didn't man succeed in splitting the
atom? If he was able to do that, he should be able to do
almost anything. He should be able to eliminate ignorance
and prejudice and war.

Ours is the challenge of Ezekiel: "Son of Man, stand
upon thy feet." We must reassert man's dignity. A generation
ago men largely abandoned faith in God for a new-found
faith in man, in a burst of optimism, rationalism, and human-
ism. Because that faith proved inadequate and unsatisfying,
because man could not provide "all the answers," this was
followed by a widespread loss of faith in man himself. Today, as a consequence, many are beset by a lack of faith in
God *and* man—a lack of faith in anything. It is a mood
which invites the "return to God." But the rediscovery of
God need not—and must not—involve a rejection of faith in

man. It should, indeed, involve a rediscovery of man as well. For the greatest achievements and potentialities of man are a reflection of his divine endowment.

Years ago the Norwegian novelist, Johann Bojer, wrote a book entitled *The Great Hunger*. In it Bojer describes a man's search for peace and happiness through self-realization. The hero of the story is a symbol—a symbol of the striving of man for truth, beauty, and goodness. The novel closes with a stirring tribute to man's uniquely creative character, which has some meaning for our day:

> Honor to thee, O spirit of Man; thou givest a soul to the world; thou settest it a goal; thou art the Hymn that lifts it into harmony. . . . Adversity can crush thee; death can blot thee out; yet art thou still unconquerable and eternal.

How Free Are We?

An object dropped from on high will fall to the ground. An object set in motion will continue in motion until its momentum is exhausted or until it encounters another object. These phenomena indicate the action of natural laws which can be tested in the laboratory and repeated at will.

If there is law at the heart of the universe, and if man is himself part of the universal scheme of things, can man escape the operation of natural law? If all the impinging factors that affect an individual in a given situation were taken into account, could we not thereby explain the individual's action in that particular situation? Is not all that we are, think, say, and do simply a product of inexorable forces that determine our destiny? How free are we?

In the literature of religion and philosophy, the problem here introduced is that of freedom of the will. Does man have free will, the capacity for determining his own fate and future? Some religions have answered in the affirmative, seeing man as a free agent; others in the negative, conceiving of man simply as the instrument of God.

The story is told of a minister who believed in pre-destination and had frequent discussions on the subject with his neighbor, who strongly disagreed. One day both left the house simultaneously, bound in opposite directions. As they met, the minister cheerily exclaimed, "It appears, Mr. Smith, that our paths were destined to cross." Thereupon his neigh-bor simply turned around and walked the other way, remark-ing, "Thus do I refute you."

Much as we might like to think that we are free agents, however, our behavior is influenced, to some extent, by both internal and external factors.

One factor that is important in determining human be-havior is, of course, heredity. Race horses have been bred for centuries. The "sport of kings" long ago recognized that the physical characteristics that make for speed and stamina in a horse can be intensified by proper breeding, by attention to hereditary factors. And we know that heredity in human beings has some influence on human characteristics—not only physical traits but mental ones as well. The Jonathan Edwards family was consistently a superior family, the Jukes family consistently inferior, to cite the classic examples.

Environmental influences also undoubtedly affect our behavior. External situations, stimuli that surround us, have an impact upon us. The importance of childhood experiences in the emotional development of the individual has often been cited: the effects of quarreling parents, a drunkard father, or a broken home. Whether one meets life and associates with others in a spirit of trust and co-operation or in a spirit of suspicion and defiance may be largely "condi-tioned" by one's early years at home. And whether we display initiative and responsibility is likely to be decided not so much by our genetic endowment as by the "handling" we have received from parents.

Does not this seem to indicate that, regardless of the age-old argument between heredity and environment, we can't win? If environment doesn't dominate us, heredity does. If heredity doesn't dominate us, then environment does. If neither by itself controls our behavior, certainly the two in combination must!

And as if this were not enough, the field of psychoanalysis indicates that much of our behavior is determined by subconscious factors, by psychological forces within ourselves that we but faintly understand and cannot easily control. The sex drive, or in its broader form, the libido, acts mightily and sometimes strangely upon us, assuming many disguises and wearing many forms. Deep-seated fears and cruelties, dark forces deriving perhaps from our animal ancestry, agitate beneath the surface of our minds, to break out in the aggressions of injustice, murder, and war. The ego seeks expression, the self status and vindication, in much that we say and do. Can we even know the mixed and subtle motivations that determine so much of our behavior? How then can we control them? Are we really the masters of our destiny? Or are we but the instruments, unwitting and perhaps even unwilling, of our subconscious drives?

The influences that affect man—hereditary, environmental, and subconscious—are indeed strong. But is this the whole of the story, and is man completely at the mercy of internal and external forces over which he has little or no control?

A woman was once asked if she believed in evolution and replied, "No, and even if it *were* true, I wouldn't believe it." We, like the woman in this story, would probably not want to believe that our lives were determined for us, even if it *were* true. But in turning our backs upon determinism—whether scientific or theological—we need not be anti-scientific or anti-religious. We need not succumb to the mechanistic approach to man as a machine; nor need we accept the belief in predestination. While recognizing that we are "creatures of the earth, earthy," and that what we do or become results, in a measure, from what we *are*, we can also recognize the divine potentialities of man and the freedom he possesses to express them. For man, beset and bedevilled by forces from within and without, displays nonetheless a degree of freedom from these forces which is remarkable.

Man is endowed with three gifts that enable him to transcend and to triumph over his environment and himself as well. The first of these is *Consciousness*, the second *Creativeness*, and the third *Conscience*.

Each of these gifts is not uniquely man's possession. All are displayed, in some limited measure and in varying degrees, by other creatures as well: the dog possesses consciousness; the beaver is creative in constructing its dams; and there are even evidences of conscience—of shame, guilt, and loyalty—in animal behavior.

It is a very low level of consciousness, if we may even recognize it as such, that prompts the amoeba, a single-celled animalcule seen only through the microscope, to move away from a foreign element introduced nearby. Yet to the degree that creatures are "conscious" of their environment, they can find food or escape danger. It may be a low level of "creativeness" that induces the bird to build its nest, yet in so doing the bird shows some capacity for *using* the *materials* of its environment to avoid being totally subject to its rigors. And it may be a low level of conscience that prompts birds and beasts to share their food with their young, or prompts a dog to save a child from a raging fire, yet these actions show some animal capacity for rising above self-interest.

To the extent that any creature possesses these attributes, he is free—free from the forces around him and the compulsions within him. But man, in the long evolutionary process, has brought these to the highest peak of development. And his is therefore the highest degree of freedom.

Man is more clearly conscious of his environment, thus better able to cope with it. He is *self*-conscious as well, possessing a measure of knowledge of himself and having the power to control his own impulses. By virtue of the apposable thumb, which distinguishes him from other creatures, he is infinitely more creative. He is able to make tools and use them: the hammer, the wedge, the wheel, and—aided by his superior consciousness of the workings of nature—cyclotrons for smashing the atom. By virtue of his higher development of conscience, he is able to establish hospitals and orphans' homes, community chests and old-age pensions, the Red Cross and the United Nations.

Let no one say that man is not free. His freedom is almost unlimited. As he further cultivates his consciousness, learning more and more about his environment and himself; as he cultivates his creativeness, composing more symphonies, building more libraries; as he harnesses that consciousness and creativeness to conscience, conquering more diseases and creating new approaches to peace, he is achieving newer and greater freedom: freedom from fear and insecurity, from want and hate, from evil and war. He is achieving ever greater freedom from the forces that enslave and brutalize men. He is achieving dignity as man.

Man's journey on this earth has been a long one, yet it has just begun. Willa Cather, in a story entitled "Before Breakfast," expresses this idea when she has her hero say, "When that first amphibious frog-toad found his water-hole dried up behind him, and jumped out to hop along till he could find another—well, he started on a long hop."

Is God Possible?

Just as we may make the mistake of belittling man in the process of exalting God, so can we fall into the error of belittling God in the process of exalting man. Seeing in man the capacity to subdue nature, conquer disease, and even control his own passions, we may be led to believe that we no longer have any need for God.

Indeed, the landscape of history is strewn with the ghosts of dead gods—gods who failed, who outlived their usefulness, who were perhaps outgrown by their followers. And there are those who believe that, even as gods have died in the past, so must God now die forever; that the time has come when we ought frankly and honestly to say that the search for God was but a characteristic of the childhood of the race, and that, now that man has come of age, he ought to rid himself entirely of this illusion of his youth, facing the world bravely and alone.

Yet the fact that man has often had inadequate conceptions of God does not mean that God Himself is an illusion, nor does it mean that we are to abandon the quest for a greater understanding of God. One might, by the same token, lose all interest in an explanation of the nature of the sun, because men at one time believed that the sun was a chariot of fire and that it entered a dark cave at night. Man's understanding of the world of nature is still incomplete; it should not be surprising that our understanding of God is also incomplete.

The idea of God, which has been so widely held by men in various ages and conditions of culture, must be treated with some deference. If we were to review the entire literature of the human race, to learn what single idea has most occupied the minds of men, it is likely that the concept of God would be most prominent. Literature deals with love and hate, with heroes and history. Yet, more usually than not, implicitly or explicitly, some awareness of God will be discovered. And on the speculative level, no other subject has lent itself so universally and frequently to discussion.

Why do men believe in God? Is God just a product of

the human fantasy, serving to rescue life from absurdity, and is the concept itself therefore rendered absurd?

Various explanations have been offered for the origin of the concept of God in the mind of man. Some have suggested that the idea of God was born of fear—fear of the lightning and thunder, fear of the unknown—fear of death. Psychologists have seen it as the expression of man's need for reassurance, his need for support. Indeed, Freud suggested that the yearning for God stems from man's experience in the womb, when he and the universe were one, when he was not yet separated from it and had not yet achieved identity as a person, and that religion is man's effort to recapture that "oceanic feeling"—to become once again not a single drop of water but a part of the sea.

Spinoza saw God as the life-principle at work in nature, regarding all of nature as the "garment of God." This view still vexes theologians who see God as "transcendent" rather than "immanent"—who refuse to see God confined within creation. Kant saw God as a force at work in nature and in the hearts of men, in terms of "the starry heavens above and the moral law within." Others have held different conceptions of God. But does anyone really know what prompts man to believe in God? Men, believing in God, have advanced many "proofs" of His existence. Yet what prompts man to believe in God may be God's belief in man—may be God Himself—granting man this insight into the ultimate nature of reality.

While we may not know *why* men have thought of God, we do know *how* men have thought of Him. And may we not, by seeing how men have thought of God, find some conception of God for ourselves?

Although men have thought of God in many ways, and expressed that thought in varied verbiage and ritual, an underlying pattern seems nonetheless discernible.

God has been thought of first as the original cause, as

the "unmoved mover" in the natural sequence of cause and effect—as the Creator of all things. This is seen in the opening sentence of Genesis: "In the beginning, God created the heavens and the earth." No attempt is made there to describe or explain God. He is assumed, as the cause of all creation. And this concept of God as the force behind creation has been part of man's thinking from the time when that sentence was first written down to our own day. Men could not conceive, to use the common illustration, of a watch without a watchmaker, of creation without a Creator. This was the most primordial response of man to the fact that the universe exists.

But that is not all. Men have also seen God in terms of process, a process at work in nature, in history, and in the life of the individual. The watchmaker, having made his watch, might then completely forsake it. If he did, the watch would first run down, then fall into disrepair, and ultimately fall apart. But men would not believe that God, having created the universe and set it in motion, would remain detached from it, content to ignore it, to let it "run down" and fall apart. Moreover, they observed that creation itself was not static but continuous. Thus they carried the concept a step further and declared that God "renews every day the work of creation"—that God is to be seen in the very processes of nature.

But could there be motion and change without purpose and goal? That would be contrary to human experience. When men walked, or ran, or moved their arms, it was with some purpose: to get some firewood, to escape a bear, to hurl a stone at an enemy. Could all the successive changes in nature be without purpose and direction? When one starts on a journey, there is a point of departure, a road to be travelled, a destination to be reached. If God was present at the start of the universe, if He is present in its operations, He must have some purpose or goal. So men learned to think of

God not only as cause, nor merely as process, but in terms of purpose—the "goal toward which creation moves."

Men today find it difficult to think of God in the same way as did the ancients. We have a greater understanding of nature, and a greater mastery over it. But can we not, even as men have done before, see God in terms of cause, of process, and of purpose?

Henri Bergson, the French philosopher of Creative Evolution, described the unfoldment of life on earth in terms of an *elan vital,* a vital force, at work in nature. He indicated that this *elan vital* has been operative in a process of continuous creation—of Creative or Emergent Evolution—from the time of the first amoeba. He concluded that the emergence of life, from simpler to more complex forms, from insentient matter to sentient man, did not take place at random, but is directional, representing a Forward Thrust at work in nature.

Le Comte du Nouy, the physiologist, in his book *Human Destiny,* speaks in much the same vein. He indicates that, mathematically speaking, it would be almost impossible for life to have emerged by pure chance. He is led to think that there is some force that rules the world, that gives life unity and meaning. There was a beginning, there has been development, and there is a future for mankind, says du Nouy. He points out that the emergence of human life from the primeval swamps, requiring untold centuries to reach its present development, is not yet completed but appears to be continuing —that life is still moving toward some higher fulfillment on the mental and spiritual level.

There is, to be sure, some difference in the language of Bergson and du Nouy and the language of Genesis, which declares that the earth and all its creatures were produced in six days. The language of Genesis is the language of Hebraic mythology; the language of Bergson and du Nouy might be called that of natural philosophy. Yet we have the same basic insight in both: that there is a creative force at work in nature;

that all of life is emergent from that source; that just as the beginning of life was no accident, man's ultimate destiny is not governed by chance.

But there is still more involved in our "justification" of religious insights of the past. For the Forward Thrust in nature must be a conscious process, directed toward a compassionate purpose. Religion will not accept a God devoid of consciousness and conscience. Yet here is the chief hurdle that modern man must leap: though able to discern consciousness and conscience in man, he finds it difficult to ascribe these qualities to God.

Our problem may arise from the fact that, in our religious literature, these qualities have often been expressed in human terms, as almost childish attempts at descriptions of God, and in the language of hyperbole, the language of poetry. The former may be resented and the latter resisted. Imaginative language is increasingly alien to our age, accustomed to the more concrete terminology of the marketplace. Yet we must recognize that we are not dealing here with weights and measures, that anthropomorphic terminology and the use of hyperbole are perhaps inevitable in an area where language is likely to be less than precise.

Perhaps the reluctance to ascribe consciousness and conscience to nature itself is due also to our inability to conceive of consciousness and conscience—if not creativeness as well—on so grand a scale, and the difficulty of discerning their action or direction in the limited time allotted to us. We find it difficult indeed to comprehend total space and total time, yet nothing less is here involved. We are in the position of a single leaf on a single twig of a single branch of a single tree: that leaf would find it difficult to comprehend the "life-plan" of the forest in which it grows. Yet ecology teaches that there is such a "life-plan" and that each of the flora and fauna in that forest is dependent for its welfare on the biological balance that exists among them all.

Some might insist that the ascription of consciousness and conscience to nature is nothing more than a wish-projection. But is this so?

If this be merely wish-projection, then it is still not to be lightly regarded. For man lives in large measure by his wishes —his wishes for himself, for his family, for society. These provide the very mainsprings of his actions. And it is indeed a tribute to man that he would wish for a universe in which power is linked with wisdom and mercy, and can see the universe in that light; that he would want to link himself with that power of wisdom and mercy and want to be a part of it— indeed, to be used by it. Men might live quite differently in a universe differently construed.

But we need not assume that this is merely wish-projection. Perhaps the "proof" of God's consciousness and conscience must forever escape us. But we find the creative principle at work in nature. And the growth of consciousness and conscience is linked with the capacity for creativeness in man and beast. Is it then too much to assume that consciousness and conscience, like creativeness, lie at the very heart of nature itself?

It is good scientific procedure to go from the known to the unknown in our quest for truth. In this case, we go from man, about whom we know at least a little, to God Whom we seek to know. Despite the danger of anthropomorphism and the limitations of language, despite the limitations of time and space with which we are confronted as observers, we are led to the conviction that human consciousness and conscience have their origin in nature.

It has, to be sure, been suggested that conscience in man is but a product of "conditioning," that man could not recognize right from wrong except by reference to the standards, the "mores" or "norms," of his society. But the study of animal behavior seems to indicate "conscience" behavior in beast as well as man; and the study of widely-scattered human societies reveals that there *are* conceptions of right and wrong among them, however widely they may differ. Is it not more likely that it is not conscience itself which is a product of conditioning, but rather the particular pattern of expression it assumes which is conditioned by the social context?

Even human consciousness has been called into question. The behaviorist school of psychology has maintained that all interpretation of human actions and reactions should be based on observation of muscular and glandular behavior. Reasoning from man to God, how can we ascribe consciousness to God when man does not really possess it? Yet awareness of the environment, and self-awareness as well, *do* emerge in man and beast, whatever the physical concomitants may be. While behaviorism has had a corrective influence on the more speculative psychology, it has not succeeded in convincing many that we are not conscious creatures.

Reverting to the evolutionary process, we might ask: Why do creativeness, consciousness, and conscience emerge in beast and man? Do these emerge as mechanisms of survival —as selective factors assuring survival? That may indeed be the case. But why do these increase from beast to man? The evolutionary process reveals the emergence of living creatures with more creativeness, more consciousness, more conscience. Why? Could not these be "chosen instruments" toward more than mere survival—toward fulfillment of some "plan"?

Religion has had the temerity to assert that these, bound up as they are with each other, are emanations from the very stuff of the universe. How else could these emerge at all? Religion further declares that if these are to be found in the very stuff of nature, this bespeaks a conscious process and compassionate purpose at work in nature itself, with man as its highest expression—as chief agent in that process, chief protagonist of that purpose.

Religion first discerned that the universe "made sense," that there is a unifying, creative force in nature. It first discerned unity and order in nature. Science, through the years, has validated that discernment, describing that unity and order in various formulae, culminating in Einstein's $E=mc^2$. What does this mean for us? Einstein himself put it this way: "God does not play dice with the universe."

But is there purpose in it, and is that purpose compassionate to man and his strivings? Religion answers in the affirmative; that both man and nature are pursuing some destiny, fulfilling some purpose or plan. Du Nouy has intimated what that purpose might be: the further development of man's mind and spirit. And science, exploring the resources of nature and human nature, may corroborate that insight, reveal more of that plan, more of the nature of God.

The cracking of the atom has provided us with the key to a new understanding of the universe. What is a chair but a constellation of atoms? What are trees, or dogs, or men but other atomic configurations? And what is an atom? Within it, we now know, are electrons, protons, and neutrons. But what is an electron? We do not know! No one has ever seen an electron. It may even be an idea. We may be led to conclude with Eddington that, in its essence, the universe is "mental." And if that be the case, it may well evidence in its workings not only a creative principle but a conscious process and compassionate purpose.

An atom is but an indication of the Universal Atom— the atom which is the universe itself. When religion declares that man's creativeness, consciousness, and conscience are but expressions of a universal creativeness, consciousness, and conscience, who is wise enough to deny it?

On Human Suffering

We are less likely to question the existence of consciousness in nature than to question nature's beneficence—its conscience or compassion. Surely, on the personal level, men daily experience grief and despair, sorrow and tragedy, and the problem of human suffering inexorably confronts us.

The classic presentation of this problem is the book of Job. Job is a thoroughly righteous man, yet he is beset by all kinds of misfortune. His friends tell him that his suffering is but proof that he has sinned and ask him to repent. But Job protests that he is innocent and does not deserve the punishment inflicted upon him.

In this story, God is testing Job, as prearranged in the prologue, to learn whether Job will love God without fear of punishment or hope of reward. Job passes this test magnificently, declaring, "Shall we accept good at the hands of the Lord, and not evil? . . . Yea, though He slay me, yet will I trust in Him."

Job "accepts" his suffering. But the question remains, *Why* do men suffer? Does this not indicate that nature is inimical, or at best indifferent, to man? How, in the face of tragedy, can we consider it compassionate?

We might begin by pointing out that there is a distinction between the type of tragedy that is manmade, and that which is sometimes called "an act of God." Take war, for example. An airplane flies over a city, dropping bombs on helpless civilians below. Is it an act of God that causes their death? Men built that airplane, men made those bombs, and human hands released them. Yet we are likely to cry out, "Why did God let it happen?" or "Why does God allow war?"

There are countries on earth where men and women suffer the direst poverty, even die of hunger on the streets. What or who is responsible for this? Is this the work of God or the result of human action—or inaction? As we look about at the suffering that exists, we must be convinced that much if not most of it is due to human cupidity and human stupidity —human greed and human ignorance.

To be sure, there are tragedies which might more nearly be described as "acts of God." A volcano erupts, and the molten lava runs down the side of the mountain, engulfing the peaceful villagers below. Or a river overflows its banks, wreaking destruction and death. These, I suppose, might be called "acts of God." Yet the people living near a volcano are not constrained to live there, and those who live near a river can move, or build a levee for protection.

So, too, with our most dreaded diseases. A person is afflicted with cancer and dies. This, of all things, might be called an "act of God." Yet if the government of the United States spent as much money annually on cancer research as it does on its military establishment, it is possible that in a few years we could eliminate cancer entirely. Have not certain diseases that once plagued man already become obsolete?

How ready we are to pass off our own responsibilities as God's responsibilities, our own failures as God's failures. I heard a minister declare, referring to the death of a child, that "God took her away." What the cause of her death was, and whether medical science was equipped to cope with her illness, I did not know. Yet I could not comprehend the bland assumption that God wanted that child more than her parents did and was cruel enough to take her from them. To accept the death of the child with resignation is one thing; to attribute that death to God's will is another.

On a philosophical level, there are various approaches to the problem. There is the attitude of the pessimist, who declares that all of life is evil, and that man is born to sorrow "as the sparks fly upward," to quote Ecclesiastes. But this is the attitude of a sick soul; it is not a healthy-minded approach to life—nor a complete one. To see only tragedy in life is just as immature as not to recognize the tragic when we see it.

Such is the case with the Christian Scientist, who takes the view that there is no suffering, no disease, or even death, that these are merely a matter of wrong thinking on our part. While we know that illness may at times be psychogenic, we are reluctant to abandon the evidence of our senses and succumb to self-delusion. We know that bacteria are real, that microbes are real, that disease and death are real.

A third approach is that of Zoroastrian dualism, which explained human suffering in terms of two forces at war in this world; the god of good and the god of evil, the god of light and the god of darkness. This serves to solve the problem very neatly, for if there are indeed two forces in conflict, then one may at times be ascendant over the other. But the Hebraic tradition and the physics of Einstein have taught us a unitary view of the universe, and we cannot accept this solution to our dilemma.

How then can we account for pain and suffering?

In the Bible we find reference to the concept that man suffers as a punishment for sin. That is why the book of Job was written: it was written to discredit that view. Today liberal religion generally rejects the association of suffering with sin. But can the idea be entirely repudiated? When we suffer from indigestion, is it not because we have been guilty of overeating? When we have a hangover, is it not because we have drunk too much? Is not suffering often the result of collective sin—sins of omission or commission? We cannot reject completely the idea that suffering is a form of punishment for sin. It often is—in spite of Job.

In the prophetic writings it is suggested that suffering may even be due to the sins of the fathers: "The fathers have eaten sour grapes, and the children's teeth are stood on edge." The later prophets sought to soften this view. But can it be completely renounced? A child is killed by an automobile while crossing the street on the way to school. Is this not due to the fact that the "town fathers" have been too negligent or niggardly to put a traffic light on that corner? Each generation *does* pay for the sins of the fathers, even "unto the third and fourth generation."

The Judeo-Christian tradition speaks also of suffering in terms of "chastisements of love." This is the idea that sorrow is visited upon us so that we may become better individuals, that we may be improved thereby, as the dross is cleaned away from metal in a crucible of fire. This may seem rash to us, and we may well reject self-improvement if it comes at the cost of suffering. But is there not some truth in this concept? Are not minority religious and racial groups, through prolonged experience with injustice, more attuned to the importance of civil liberties? And this is true on an individual level as well: a couple who have lost a child may devote their lives to working with children; an industrialist whose wife has died of leukemia may devote his fortune to cancer research.

There *is* suffering in the world, and tragedy *is* real for its victim. Recently an airplane crashed, killing all of its occupants. Among them was a young man, twenty-six years of age, the son of a colleague of mine. Why should he and they have had to die?

This is indeed a troublesome question, and no answer is likely to prove completely satisfactory to those who have suffered the loss of a dear one. Yet Maimonides, a twelfth-century philosopher, comes as close to an answer as we are likely to get: that man is imperfect, and matter is imperfect; that God works in and through imperfect man and matter.

The materials that went into the construction of the plane that crashed were not perfect, the men who made it were not perfect, the men who guided that plane to its tragic destiny were not perfect, the atmospheric conditions were not perfect, nor were they perfectly understood. In a profound sense, the crash of that plane was not an accident; it was in the very nature of things.

That plane can serve as a symbol. Men can build better

planes, be better pilots, learn more about atmospheric conditions. Surely, there are fewer crashes now than in the infancy of aviation, and there will be fewer still in the future. There will be fewer deaths from cancer and heart disease and other ailments that now afflict mankind, as there are now fewer deaths from polio, when men devote their time, their talent, and their treasure to these ends.

In spite of tragedy, it may be that the universe is not indifferent to man's aims; it may be that man is indifferent to God's. An old rabbinic statement declares that suffering was put into the world so that man could strive to remove it. This may indeed be God's will—and our task here on earth.

We have been given the materials to work with. For if there is suffering in the world, is there not good as well? And is this not the greater marvel—that out of inert matter goodness should arise? There is good in nature: in the sunlit sky and the fruited plains, in the medicinal molds and in the power that is locked in the atom. There is good in man as well: in his capacity for love and loyalty, for tenderness and affection, for sympathy and compassion.

There is a force for good at work in this universe. And man is uniquely allied to that force. He must work with it, and allow it to work through him. Martin Buber, the contemporary religious philosopher, tells the story of a sage who walked into a room where his disciples were engaged in study. He asked them: "Where is God to be found?" After a moment of hesitation, one of them replied: "The whole earth is full of His glory." But the master answered: "Wherever men let Him in." George Eliot has Stradivarius put it this way:

'Tis God gives skill,
But not without men's hands: He could not make
Antonio Stradivari's violins
Without Antonio.

Is Death the End?

We learn rather early in life that all living things have an end as well as a beginning. This fact slowly works its way into our consciousness, and we somehow come to terms with it. Indeed, we plan accordingly: we provide for our retirement, we take out insurance policies and write wills for the disposal of our estates.

To go through life with never a thought to death is to live in a world of fantasy. But to go through life with the fear of death is to create for oneself a world of misery. Since death is but a part of life, one must learn not to see life from the perspective of death but to see death itself from the perspective of life. While the realities of life do not preclude the ever-present possibility of death, the reality of death should not negate the possibilities of life.

Yet death does come, sometimes tragically, when the potentialities of life have hardly been tested. Especially trying is the death of a loved one with whom we have been associated long and intimately, with whom we have, in a very real sense, shared our lives. Surely it is as if a part of us were torn away, for we give something of ourselves to those who are closest to us, and they return something of themselves to us. The encounter with death has prompted man from the beginnings of human history to ask, "Is death the end?" and to seek some satisfying answer.

Although a complete answer has not yet been provided, and perhaps never will, the religions of the world have offered varying conceptions of the nature of death. There are Eastern religions, for example, which teach the doctrine of metempsychosis, the transmigration of souls. This is the belief that, in some previous incarnation, each of us has been a different person, or some other creature, and that when this life is over we take on another form, another body, and live once again here on earth.

The major religions of the West have not been hospitable

to this idea. They have conceived of death rather as the release of the soul, or essence, or personality of man from his earthly form, and the survival of that soul, essence or personality in some non-corporeal existence, as "spirit." Yet even the concept of "spiritual" survival has lent itself to varied interpretation. To the more orthodox, it may convey a wraith-like existence, in less than corporeal form, but retaining somehow the aspects and dimensions of that form. To the more liberal, "spiritual" survival may mean something far different from that.

Liberal religionists generally agree on three approaches to immortality. The first of these is the immortality we achieve through our children, a kind of "biological" immortality. And such immortality is certainly real, for genetically we do not die if we leave children. Indeed, from a biological point of view, we are but the temporary carriers of the germ plasm which is transmitted through us to those who follow.

Second, there is the immortality of the words we speak and the deeds we perform, whose influence upon others gives us a "social" immortality. Each of us is the recipient of many influences from many sources. The influence of a parent, a teacher, a friend, does not die with the death of that person but continues to live in us. Each of us somehow keeps alive some part of the personality of those whose lives touched ours.

Third, there is the immortality achieved through memory, a kind of "psychological" immortality, for we survive in the *memory* of others even after death. Surely the remembered image of the departed has a quality of reality, a kind of "existence" that cannot be completely denied. Maurice Maeterlinck, in a letter to Mrs. Thomas Kearney Glenn, once expressed this idea most beautifully, emphasizing the need to keep alive our memories of the dead:

> . . . There are no dead because memory brings them back when our thoughts visit them. Forgetting is the only possible form of annihilation. Let us learn not to for-

get. . . . The death of memories is a second death more cruel than the first. . . . If we had no memories, if we had no more dead behind us, if everything which we think dead did not live any longer in us, what would remain for us, and what would we be? . . . We are the cemetery of our dead, but it is a living cemetery, animated like a children's village in a fairy tale.

All the above forms of survival are unquestionable. Surely we "survive" in our children, in the influence of our words and deeds on the lives of others, and in the memories of those we leave behind. Yet ancient insights, while clothed in the language of hyperbole and metaphor, are not entirely valueless and spurious; immortality may yet be more real and personal than the biological, social, or psychological immortality here alluded to. As William James has pointed out, if there can be no proof of immortality, there can be no disproof of it, and therefore the "will to believe," the eternal human hunger for the assurance that the dead somehow survive, need not be rejected, though we know not what form that survival may take.

We do not know all there is to know about the universe we live in or about man's individual or collective destiny, and perhaps we never will. But we do know that, in nature's economy, none of the elements that make up the human body is lost. These elements are simply released to assume other forms, to take on other attachments. "They are gone to feed the roses," as Edna St. Vincent Millay expressed it. Our lives as individuals, as persons, may end but only once again to become a part of universal life. Here perhaps is the source of the Eastern concept of the transmigration of souls, of the Western concept of the soul's return to its Creator. Nothing in nature is lost—it is only transformed.

Is this true only on a "physical" level? What *is* "physical"? We have begun to discover that all reality is one, that we cannot easily distinguish between motion and matter,

matter and energy. Can we then distinguish between body and soul, flesh and spirit?

Men have long thought that only the body died, while the spirit was released. Must we now, knowing that there is no physical death but only transformation, only physical release, think that only the *spirit* dies? This would be paradoxical indeed, a strange inversion of what men have so long believed. And, like the belief that only the body dies, it would perpetuate that dualism which sees matter and energy, body and soul, as separate entities—a dualism no longer tenable.

If the one does not really die, but is only transformed, may this not be true of the other? If so, we should perhaps view with a more open mind the whole realm of psychic phenomena. Unfortunately this field has had very little scientific investigation, and we have no clear light on the subject.

In the absence of such knowledge, however, if we see in a dream the form of one we loved, or waking, seem to hear some admonition through his voice, we ought not to lose ourselves in fantasies about a world we have not seen. We ought rather to regard this as striking evidence of the love which bound him to us.

Whatever may await us when the cord of life is severed, mature faith does not seek to storm the gates of heaven. It seeks not so much to explain our dying as to transform our living, to link our lives with the life-asserting, life-enhancing forces that surround us. As we relate ourselves to that which is eternal, to that which has meaning, our own lives share in that meaning and death becomes less real or important. Bernard Berenson, approaching eighty, put it this way:

> Now I am in the decline of my eighth decade, and live so much more in the people, the books, the works of art, the landscape than in my own skin, that of self . . . little is left over. A complete life may be one ending in so full an identification with the not-self that there is no self left to die.

The Language of Faith

Some time ago, I had occasion to spend several days on a sailboat as a guest of the owner. During the course of the voyage, I was intrigued to learn of the extensive vocabulary of terms involved in sailing—terms with which I had been previously unacquainted.

Such terms as "fore" and "aft," "leeward," "starboard," "port," "fors'l," "mains'l," "mizzen"—familiar to many a landlubber—represent only a fraction of the vocabulary with which the sailing man is at home. And anyone who even pretends to have any acquaintance with sailing ships must master this vocabulary of ship and sea.

Much the same thing is true in any field of human interest and endeavor, for each, to some degree, involves a unique vocabulary, best known and understood by those most at home in that field. In the various sports, such assorted devices are used for hitting a ball as a stick, a bat, a mallet, and a racket. One would have to know something about each of the sports involved to know in which of them these specific objects are used.

The field of religion too has its own vocabulary—a vocabulary that has developed through the centuries of religious thought and aspiration. Some of these terms, like some of the terms involved in sailing and other sports, are fairly familiar to most people. Others are much less familiar and known only to the devotee. What serves to make the vocabulary of religion the more difficult to master, however, is the fact that its terms deal with concepts or ideas rather than with things. For we deal here with intangibles which cannot be seen or felt through the usual avenues of sense perception.

It is relatively easy to learn what a mains'l is, or what a baseball bat looks like. We have but to be shown the objects, see them in use, and we become familiar with them. We can even handle them and get the "feel" of them. To be sure, there are differences between one mains'l and another (some, for example, are made of nylon, and not all of them are cut alike) and even between baseball bats (which may vary in weight and length). But the shape of the object, the appearance of it, and the purpose for which it is used can be readily understood.

The language of faith, the vocabulary of religion, is somewhat more involved. Even the terms that are best known—"God," the "soul," to name but two—are not necessarily well understood. The "soul" can be construed in a narrow and literal sense as something nearly substantial. (Indeed, men once thought the soul resided in the breath and upon death was expelled from the body in almost physical form.) Yet the same term can be used in a completely figurative and poetic sense. And the same is true of the term "God."

The meaning inherent in the terminology of religion is likely to be determined not so much by the perception as by the apperception of the hearer or reader; that is, not so much what he finds *in* it as what he brings *to* it. Unless, in using the term, a writer or speaker makes every effort to explain just how he is using it, just how he wants it understood, each will understand it in his own way, in accordance with his previous experience or lack of experience with that term.

How many attempts have been made through the centuries to define God and the soul! Yet where is the definition of these terms that is today universally accepted after all these attempts? How can we even go about the effort to define them?

Any definition involves two things: the *genus proximum* and the *differentia specifica*: the naming of the larger category to which the object belongs and the specific way in which the particular object differs from other items in that category. Thus, a bicycle is a two-wheeled vehicle. As a "vehicle," it belongs in the same category as the automobile, tricycle, or trolley-car. But since we have said it is "two-wheeled," a specific type of vehicle is described, different from the others. But into what "general category" can we place God or the soul? And what "specific character" would distinguish these from other members of that category? Following the classic requirement for achieving a definition, none would seem possible.

This is not necessarily true in dealing with other ideas. While ideas are more difficult to define than things, they do lend themselves to definition. Thus, "summer" is the "hot season," summer being first a season, then specifically characterized by heat. Even love may be defined, as an "emotion of sympathetic concern." Emotions, as a category, are at least somewhat understood, and sympathetic concern is at least one way of distinguishing this particular emotion from others. Even the "purple cow," which is pure fantasy, can be defined, for we have all seen cows and are familiar with the color purple, so that we can actually construct an image of a purple cow in our minds.

Since there is no "general category" nor "specific differential" for God, men have approached the definition of God differently: through descriptive language, through attributes. God is, for example, the Lord, the Creator, the Almighty, the All-Powerful, the All-Wise, the All-Knowing, the King of kings, the Rock of our salvation. He is a Loving Father, merciful, just; He is infinite and eternal, yet "near unto those who call upon Him." He is to be found in the lightning and thunder, yet also within the heart of man.

But all these characterizations, for all their number and descriptiveness, somehow fall short of constituting a definition. Indeed, some of the attributes ascribed to God may be expressions of human qualities and human experiences. Such terms as "Lord" or "King" indicate reverence for a master, in this case a more-than-earthly Master. Such terms as "All-Wise," "All-Powerful," may express the limitations of our own wisdom and power; terms like "the Infinite" and "the Eternal" express our own finitude. But how else can we think of God—or of anything—except in terms of our apperceptions, in terms of our human associations?

Man, earth-bound and mortal, has always evidenced a sense of the unlimited and the eternal. Man, faltering and imperfect, has evidenced an awareness of the possibility of intellectual and moral perfection. All this he has tried to convey in the language of faith. Bound by the very inadequacy of language, he has selected from his reservoir of words those that best served to describe the paradox of his own wisdom and ignorance, his own strength and weakness, his own capacity for tenderness and tyranny, to describe, by contrast and comparison, One Who was All-Wise, All-Powerful and All-Merciful.

The language of faith is therefore inevitably the language of hyperbole, of metaphor and simile—the language of poetry, the language of the heart. Thus God is still described as the King of kings in an age when kings are disappearing from the earth; as a Shepherd in an age of automobiles and television. He is characterized as a Heavenly Father in an age when the heavens themselves have been penetrated by planes and the concept of "father" is entangled with the Oedipus Complex.

Yet there is a truth that lies in poetry, an intimation of realities that lie beyond the senses. And it is by that truth and those realities, even more than by the grosser and more obvious truths and realities of daily experience, that man lives on this earth. Our expressions of religious insight are restricted by the limitations of language itself, but these insights are nonetheless genuine. Beneath the metaphor there is meaning; behind the simile there is sense; within the poetry there is profundity.

A Universal Faith?

Men of good will have often wondered why the ethics of religion should so often have been lost sight of in the concern over creedal differences, why so-called religious men have so often acted irreligiously toward one another. Surely we must be aware that religion, teaching brotherhood and love, has sometimes served as a divisive force in the lives of men, causing them too often to look upon one another with suspicion and even hostility.

Some have concluded that it might be best to eliminate religion entirely, so that this area of friction between men would no longer exist. "Should we not simply scrap religion and recognize that, instead of being members of one denomination or another, we are simply all human beings?" they have asked. But that would be like "throwing out the baby with the bath," when it is only the bath water we want to throw out. It would be like discarding the use of fire, which is necessary to cook our food and to keep us warm in winter, simply because fire is capable of burning down the house we live in.

To be sure, religion can be abused. Yet those who say, "Let us scrap religion," might just as well jettison all of our tenderest human emotions, because they too can be abused. Pity, for example, is indeed a noble sentiment. Yet Stefan Zweig, in a novel entitled *Beware of Pity*, indicates how it can become a destructive force. He tells the story of a young soldier who was treated well by his colonel, invited into his house, given fine food and drink, until he felt himself a member of the household. The colonel had an invalid daughter, to whom, out of compassion, the young man paid special attention, remembering her birthday, bringing her flowers, and the like. But she misunderstood his motives and thought he was in love with her. And, when the time came for him to move on, she committed suicide.

Though the spirit of compassion—of pity—is sublime,

it must be guided by reason. This is true even of the tender emotion of love. For even love may be abused. You may remember reading, or seeing the film, *My Son, My Son*. This was the story of a father who loved his son dearly, but unwisely. He protected him from all possible harm, intervened when the boy got into trouble, and even lied for him. Finally, the boy committed murder, and the father could not help him; he was sentenced to die. It was only then that the father recognized how his love had actually destroyed his son, for that love had been too protective.

Religious feeling possesses the same ambivalent potential: it has the capacity for eliciting from human beings the noblest ideals and actions. Yet, if not guided by reason, it may lead men to hate, and even kill. There have, for example, been "religious wars," though the very concept of a "religious war" should be a contradiction in terms. And men have been burned at the stake because of religious differences. But we do not scrap pity or love because they are sometimes unwisely understood or applied; nor need we scrap religion because it can be misunderstood or misapplied.

Thus it is that men who have been interested in religion, and who have also been interested in bridging the gaps that divide men from one another, sometimes raise another question, "Why can't we have a universal religion—a religion that would unite rather than separate men, a religion that would express their noblest aspirations and translate their loftiest ideals into living realities?" This question can be raised sincerely; the question is quite valid. For a universal faith might express what is best in each religion, and draw men closer together.

The idea of a universal religion must indeed have intrigued all of us at one time or another. We all recognize, if we take the trouble to examine religion at all, that there is in every religion an inner core of moral teaching. And we all recognize that this inner core of moral teaching serves somehow as a common denominator of all religions, whatever the creed or form of expression.

It is fascinating to discover, for example, that while Jesus expressed the Golden Rule in the words, "Do unto others as you would have others do unto you," somewhat the same idea was expressed by the gentle Rabbi Hillel, in the words, "What is hateful unto you, do not unto another," just a generation before the time of Jesus. And we find a similar idea developed by Confucius fully five centuries earlier, and in the religion of Zoroaster. Is it not remarkable that, on the moral level, the religions of the world have so very much in common?

But to say that there is a common core of morality inherent in all religions does not of itself make a universal faith either feasible or desirable. Gertrude Stein once said, "Everything is the same and everything is different." There is a common humanity in all men, yet each is an individual. And if all religions are the same, they too are nonetheless different.

In this age of the atom, we are learning to think broadly of humanity, and we are beginning to see that all men have common needs, common fears, and common hopes. The recognition that we are all human beings, regardless of nationality, race, or religion, is all to the good. Yet it should be remembered that while all people are human beings, there are no people who can be designated *simply* as human beings. There are only Frenchmen, Englishmen, Americans, Chinese, and the like.

So too with the possibility of a universal religion. "The religions of mankind," to paraphrase Gertrude Stein, "are all the same, yet they are all different." Just as there are no "men" in the abstract, only Kelly, Anastasio, and Cohen, no "humanity" in the abstract, only Frenchmen, Iranians, Americans, and Chinese, so there is no "religion" in the abstract, only Christianity, Judaism, Mohammedanism, and Confucianism. Kelly is Kelly because he is descended of the Kellys; the

Frenchman is a Frenchman because he stems from the French; and the Christian is a Christian because he is a product of the Christian tradition.

The attempt to achieve a united humanity without regard for the linguistic, cultural, economic, and industrial differences that exist, for example, between the Americans and Siamese, would be foolish and foredoomed to failure. The United Nations does not insist that member nations follow the same customs or have the same type of government. It does not strive for uniformity but for unity. Similarly, the attempt to achieve a world religion without regard to the differences that exist, say, between the Jewish and Buddhist traditions, would be equally unsuccessful because it would be equally unrealistic.

Attempts to create a universal religion have actually been made: the Baha'i movement, and the Ethical Culture movement, perhaps. Yet while one may admire the idealism that motivates the founders of these faiths, one must recognize that religions, like languages, are not really "made" but are born, or emerge, out of a given time and place, an ethnic group, a cultural milieu, as a living force in the lives of men, as a synthesis of the experiences and aspirations of that group and that era. That is why artificial attempts at formulating universal religions (or international languages) in our day, noble as they may be, have not won wide followings.

But there is more than the question of *feasibility* of a universal religion involved. There is also the question whether such a world religion is really *desirable*.

Walt Whitman pointed out several generations back that America is "not a nation, but a nation of nations." There have always been those who would make of this nation of nations a "melting-pot" in which group characteristics would be lost in a common brew and in which even divergencies of opinion would be melted down. But we have learned to think of America in terms of "cultural pluralism" rather than the "melting-pot." We do not want a nation of "faceless" or "thoughtless" men. We have learned that differences can be enriching to the material and spiritual growth of this nation.

Indeed, what makes America great, and unique among the nations, is the amazing variety of ethnic groups in this country, the successful orchestration of these different elements within the population, and the tremendous outpouring of the diversified gifts of mind and spirit from all these divergent elements, in science and technology, in industry and the arts, that today give America pre-eminence in almost every field of human endeavor.

This may serve as an analogy of what we might expect of the religions of the world; not that each be stripped of its uniqueness, but that each contribute something of its uniqueness to the total quest for religious truth; not that all be made to fit the Procrustean bed of a universal faith, but that each, as a truly living faith, discover to the fullest its own unique capacity to contribute to our understanding of all religion. For, in a sense, each religion sees truth "as in a glass, darkly," perceiving but part of the spiritual truth by which men must live, or perceiving that truth through its own historic coloration.

Judaism and Christianity have helped to shape the values of our Western civilization and can still contribute mightily to this civilization. And if we knew more about the religions of the Eastern world, we would find in them certain emphases and overtones which might serve to enrich our appreciation of the possibilities of religion even further. In each of these traditions we have vast treasures of religious experience and expression which can somehow serve to enlarge and deepen our own.

In a symphony orchestra, there is no need for the violin to play the part of the oboe; no need for the flute to play the part of the cello. Possessing different tones and playing different notes, each is nonetheless playing the same composition. With proper orchestration, each can contribute to the perfect rendition of the same divine symphony, performing in concerted effort under the leadership of the same master musician.

3

INTERPRETING TRADITION

The Book of Books

In the attempt to achieve religious maturity, we cannot bypass the Bible, the greatest of all reservoirs of religious thought through the ages. The Bible has always been, and remains today, the world's best seller, perennially outselling every book on the market. Paradoxically, however, it is probably the world's most misunderstood book.

Having served for centuries as the basis of the religious beliefs of many divergent groups, it has been subjected to many different interpretations in support of those beliefs. "Even the devil can quote Scripture," runs the old adage. And the Bible has been used to sustain strange causes. During the Civil War, there were ministers who supported slavery on the ground of Scriptural citations, while others used Biblical texts to oppose it. Men have spoken for and against the prohibition of alcoholic beverages, turning to the Bible for justification of their positions.

During the Second World War, the minister of a large and influential congregation, alarmed at the possibility that Americans might soon be eating horse-meat because of the wartime meat shortage, declared, "To eat the flesh of a horse is contrary to the teachings of the Bible, for the Bible teaches that we may eat only such animals as have split hooves and chew their cud." He quite forgot that the Bible also pro-

61

hibits—far more specifically—the eating of swine's flesh.
And, since neither he nor the members of his congregation
were Orthodox Jews, I assume they *did* eat that.

When I was a boy a trial took place in Dayton, Tennessee, which became famous as the Dayton Monkey Trial. The
case was made the subject of the Broadway play, *Inherit the
Wind*. It involved a Tennessee school-teacher named Scopes
who was fired from his job because he was allegedly teaching
evolution. The case was brought to trial, with Clarence
Darrow, the great agnostic, defending Scopes, and William
Jennings Bryan, the distinguished fundamentalist, opposing
him.

At one point Darrow asked Bryan whether he believed
that the whale actually swallowed Jonah, and Bryan replied
that he did. Then Darrow asked whether Bryan would believe
that Jonah swallowed the whale if that were in the Bible, and
Bryan once again answered in the affirmative, forced into
that position by his literal acceptance of the Bible.

What is most disconcerting about this contretemps is the
fact that both of these men failed to understand the Bible,
failed to get at the real truth inherent in the story of Jonah.
For the writer of the story of this reluctant prophet meant to
convey the message of compassion—compassion even for the
sinful people of Nineveh! The need for compassion in human
relations is a spiritual truth, yet this religious message of that
precious little book escaped both the agnostic and the
religionist!

Ardent believer and outspoken skeptic are likely to make
the same mistake: they both are likely to miss the point. They
really are brothers under the skin and share a common attitude toward the Bible: the feeling that if errors, contradic-
tions, or improbabilities are found in it, the Bible, and thereby
religion itself, is undermined.

Thus the ardent believer, motivated by genuine if misapplied piety, feels constrained to defend the Bible against

its detractors by freezing it with the rigidity of literalness and reducing its viability as a living influence, missing the message it contains. The outspoken skeptic, as the champion of truth and clarity of thought, nobly motivated but equally misguided, feels impelled to point out its inaccuracies and inadequacies and loses himself in the trees, failing to see the forest, failing to see the greater significance of the Bible.

What *is* the Bible? It is a book, one is tempted to reply. Yet the Bible is more than a book, it is a whole library of books. It is the most impressive collection of books man has ever possessed, for it represents the experiences and insights of more than a thousand years of human life and thought. It is the greatest body of literature ever composed, for it represents man's confrontation with himself, with his fellow-man, and with the very source of his being.

In a sense, the Bible is an anthology. Suppose, for the sake of analogy, a careful selection were made of the best writing produced in the entire period of British literary history, roughly a thousand years. We might include the legend of Beowulf, crude and mythological in character, the tales of King Arthur and his knights, the plays of Shakespeare, the poetry of Byron, Keats, and Shelley, and the work of such men as Bernard Shaw, coming down to our own time. This anthology would contain some of the legends, poetry, plays, and essays produced by the British and reflect a thousand years of growth in British civilization.

There are, of course, such anthologies of English literature, and most of us are familiar with at least some of this material. English professors have not stopped assigning the reading of Beowulf because they suspect that the dragons Beowulf slew were only mythological in character. We have not stopped reading the stories of King Arthur because we doubt that Sir Launcelot and Queen Guinevere ever lived. We do not disdain the plays of Shakespeare because he borrowed some of his plots from Bocaccio and others; because of the geographical inaccuracies he commits, such as ascribing a seacoast to Bohemia, an inland nation; or because he sometimes mixes his metaphors, as when he speaks of taking up "arms against a sea of trouble."

Byron and Shelley lived in a romantic era, while we live in an industrial age, but have we discarded their poetry for this reason? We continue to read such things because they are part of that literary heritage which has gone into the making of our own, part of a civilization that has contributed something to ours, and because they have intrinsic beauty and worth as expressions of the creative human spirit. And if all this be true of English literature, how much more true it is of the Bible.

In the Bible we find mythological material, such as the story of the creation of the world, the tale of Adam and Eve, and the saga of Noah and the flood. In the Bible we have also history, the account of the exodus from Egypt, the settlement of Canaan, the rise of the kings and prophets. In the Bible we find poetry as well, from the exotic love poem, the Song of Songs, to the sublimely spiritual poetry of the Psalms which scale the ladder of human emotions from abject despair to triumphant exaltation.

In the Bible we find philosophy, addressing itself to the fundamental questions of life, such as the book of Job on the question of Good and Evil, and the book of Ecclesiastes on the question of the worthwhileness of life itself. In the Bible we find law, for we are told how to determine the responsibility if an ox has gored a man, or if a man is found murdered in a public place. And in the Bible we find, above all, morality, in the Ten Commandments and in the injunction "Thou shalt love thy neighbor as thyself."

An anthology? Yes, a wonderful anthology. This particular anthology has been read by more human beings than any other and has had a greater influence than any other. It has given men serenity and inner peace; it has also roused

them to revolt. It has taught men to be meek; it has also led
them to war. It has taught them tenderness; yet it has sometimes led them to hate. Nothing during the past two thousand
years has so consistently and so profoundly affected men's
thoughts and actions. Without it, we would not have Michel-
angelo's Moses, the oratorios of Handel, or Milton's "Paradise Lost." Without it, all the arts would be the poorer.

To art, to music, to poetry, the Bible has served as a
fertile source of inspiration. It has had a profound impact on
our habits of thought and, through the English translation,
upon our habits of speech. It has influenced our conceptions
of morality and has penetrated our system of laws. The Bible
is the only anthology that can be accepted with reverence or
rejected with wrath but cannot be ignored.

Yet the Bible is more than an anthology, for the term
does not fully describe its character. If the Bible is an anthology in that it contains such divergent types of literary
material, covering so long a period in human history; and if
it has had so profound an impact on the lives of men and on
the arts of civilization, that alone does not *constitute* its
uniqueness.

What is truly unique about this anthology is the fact
that, despite its variety of expression, and despite the time
covered in its composition, there is a single thread that runs
through it all, that gives it unity. It is many books, yet it is,
in a deeper sense, one book. What is the thread that binds it
together? The quest for a definition of man's place in God's
world. What makes the Bible sublime is that it is a record
of man's attempt to relate himself to the universe, reaching
inward to discover his own identity, outward to link himself
with the entire human family, and upward to relate himself
to the very source of life.

And so we come full circle, back to where we started.
The Bible is a religious book; indeed, it is *the* religious book
par excellence. In it man seeks meaning in life: in nature, in

history, in all of his human relationships, and in the deepest struggles and experiences of the human heart, arriving at moral and social insights, levels of human hope and aspiration, that make him indeed "but little lower than the angels."

The Meaning of Myth

Who the first man was, and how he actually came into being, will probably always remain unanswered questions. It is significant that the Hebrew Bible makes no real attempt to name the first man and woman, the name Adam being but a play on the word *adamah*, meaning earth, because he was taken from the earth, and the name Eve being a variant of the Hebrew word for life, because she was to be the mother of all the living. In other words, their very names are symbolic in character! And it is fascinating that Maimonides observed that the story of Adam and Eve and the serpent was not to be regarded as factual but rather as allegorical.

Almost eight centuries later, in 1941, the Doctrinal Commission of the Church of England declared, "We regard the story of Genesis as entirely symbolical." This statement and the statement of Maimonides are interesting for two reasons: not only do they deny the historical authenticity of the story of Genesis, but they imply that there are other areas of meaning in that story.

What are those meanings? At the very least, the story of Genesis tells us what men once thought about the beginnings of the world and man. But more than that, in the story they have left us, they reveal the element of intellectual curiosity. We can feel almost a sense of pride in these ancients who lived so long ago yet rose above the level of brutish complacency, displaying indeed Promethean temerity in trying to wrest from the universe its deepest secrets. And we can feel just a little bit humble that we, so many centuries later, have not yet fully discovered the answers.

The universe as represented in the book of Genesis was indeed much simpler than the universe as we now know it, with its galaxies of stars and immensities of space. The origins of the earth are somewhat differently presented in that fascinating document from the way in which we now believe the earth was formed in, say, "the nebular hypothesis," the theory that all the planets were once part of the sun. It seems incomprehensible to us that the world could have come into being in six days in view of the researches and discoveries in the fields of geology and archaeology. Moreover, in the light of the theory of evolution, it seems naive to suppose that man was created at a single moment, out of the dust of the earth, and Eve from one of his ribs.

But it is only the college sophomore who would stop there. The more thoughtful would be intrigued that man long ago learned to ask questions, that he was not content, like the other creatures on earth, to live, to procreate and die; that he was always and interminably asking the questions How? and Why?

How did the earth come into being? What was the order of creation? This was the answer the ancients gave: Day and night; then the heavens, earth, and sea; the grass of the field; sun, moon, and stars; the fish of the sea; the animals of the land, the birds of the air; and finally Man. This was their conception of the order of creation.

Why must man, alone of all creatures on earth, eat bread by the sweat of his brow? The ancients answered: Because God had cursed the earth on his account, so that it would not yield its bounty without toil. Why could man not live forever? Because he had sinned. Why must woman endure pain in childbirth? Because she allowed herself to be tempted. These were their answers to some deep and searching questions.

All this does not sound very scientific. Yet man long ago was already something of a scientist. He was already making observations, asking questions about what he observed, and attempting an explanation. Is not this the heart of the scientific method? To be sure, the answers given must be classified as mythology, but mythology is the earliest form of science.

Much more recently than the writing of Genesis, mythology has indeed passed for science. It was not too long ago in the history of mankind that men sought the philosopher's stone which would transmute base metals into gold. It was not too long ago in the history of the human race that man studied the stars in the belief that they had some influence on human behavior. Some of the most important discoveries in astronomy were made by men who thought the stars determined our destiny. Even today, there are many who "follow the stars" in their personal affairs: when a popular newspaper omitted its astrology column one day, it had thousands of complaints from readers!

When I was a child at the close of the First World War, our family physician advised that we wear camphor bags around our necks to escape the influenza epidemic. Subsequent medical discoveries indicate that if my family survived that epidemic it was not because of the camphor bags at all.

The human quest for truth is a constant quest; men asked questions long ago, and are still asking them. The science of one generation may become the superstition of the next, and one must see the human advance as a long, laborious, yet nonetheless glorious adventure.

The story of Genesis is symbolic of that eternal quest; symbolic of man's unwillingness to remain at the level of the beast in intelligence, imagination or conscience; symbolic also of man's desire to link himself with the rest of creation, through the comprehension of that single principle which animates man and nature. Viewed in this light, the story of Genesis is a record of the struggle of man's mind in quest of knowledge, man's conscience in quest of morality, man's spirit

in quest of its source. It is the record of man turning to his
origins to discover his destiny.

There is symbolism in the story of Cain and Abel in the
light of which the question, Whom did Cain marry? is rendered trivial. From the beginning of human life on this planet
there has been wickedness and evil. When Cain slew Abel,
brother slew brother—as men have been doing ever since.
And the voice of God speaks now, as it did then, to those
who can hear it. We are admonished still, as was Cain in this
precious narrative, that sin "crouches at the door," but that
we may "rule over it." And what profound symbolism lies
in the fact that Cain hid from God. Man is a creature of conscience; he knows when he has done wrong. Yet how often
he tries, like Cain, to "hide from God."

There is further symbolism inherent in the Genesis
material which can be significant for today and for all time.
There is symbolism in the fact that man was the last of the
creatures on earth to come into being, for man is here presented as the very culmination of creation, a creature of
infinite dignity and worth. Man alone is created singly in the
Biblical narrative; the verb used in connection with his creation is different from that used in other connections; and he
is, in the story of Genesis, created "in the image of God."

There is powerful symbolism in the idea that man was
created in the image of God. This may very well be the most
brilliant act of presumption ever perpetrated by man. But
think of what is implied! Power, wisdom, and goodness are
ascribed to man, who shares the very attributes of divinity.
As God is a creator, so is man a creator! This means that he
can change the character of the world he inhabits. He can
eliminate disease, poverty, and war. He can conquer hatred,
fear, and envy. Because he possesses the divine spark of intelligence and morality, because he himself is a creator, he
can accomplish all this if he wills it.

So too with the story of the Garden of Eden. Man is living in a world that is governed by ineffable law by which he must abide, and science seeks to discover its operations. But the life of mankind is also governed by a moral law, no less inexorable: love breeds love, and hate breeds hate. Man, understanding that law and learning to live by it, can indeed live in a Garden of Eden; he can make this world his paradise. But man, defying the moral law and failing to live by it, ostracizes himself, is ejected and exiled; the Garden of Eden is taken from him. He is given the power of choice, the power to comply or not to comply with the demands of divinity. He can determine his own destiny on earth. This is the challenging symbolism of the story.

Mythology is not pure fantasy. Mythology too can have meaning. It is important that we read it correctly, understanding the truths it transmits.

The Matter of Miracles

The association of the miraculous with religion is almost universal, and of long standing. From the viewpoint of the devout, the element of the miraculous in religion, the suspension of the very laws of nature on behalf of some person or cause, is the strongest evidence of the existence of a Power behind the universe Who, having first established these laws, can at will set them aside.

It is a position which seems to need no defense. If there is in this world a force which is not only all-powerful but also concerned with the fate of men and nations, why should it be necessary to explain the element of the miraculous in religion? Surely that Power within the universe is the master, not the slave, of these laws of nature, and can use them or dismiss them in the achievement of His purpose!

But the more critical are not thus easily persuaded of the possibility of miracles. Science operates on the premise that this is a world of law and that the laws governing the universe are fixed laws. If the laws of the physical universe could be suspended from time to time, the investigations of science would be rendered meaningless. Certain calculations, for example, are based on the fact that a falling body will accelerate at the rate of thirty-two feet per second every second while falling. Should there be even the slightest chance that this law of gravity would momentarily cease to operate, all of our knowledge based upon its operation and all experiments based on that knowledge would be useless.

Where the laws of nature do not seem to be operating with consistency, the scientist is led to check the data with which he is working to determine their accuracy, or the instruments he is using to determine their reliability. If, after that, he still finds some inconsistency, he is compelled to revise and improve his understanding of these natural laws themselves, for he can only assume that he has not understood them completely. He is convinced that this universe is subject to law and is determined to discover its nature. If, as Hamlet says to his friend, "There are more things in heaven and earth, Horatio, than are dreamt of in your philosophy," he seeks to know them too, and to extend his knowledge still further. In the realm of miracles, the man of science is, and must remain, unconvinced.

The critical mind may find several approaches to the matter of miracles. First, the possibility that the events described never really happened but were inventions of man's own imagination. Second, that something did take place which to the untrained observer seemed miraculous because he had not sufficient knowledge to comprehend it. Third, that in the process of transmission from person to person and from generation to generation, the account itself was distorted.

As to the first possibility, we know that events can be invented, or novels could not be written. As to the second, we know how difficult it is to get witnesses to agree on what they saw when an automobile accident has taken place and how divergent their testimony is likely to be. And as to the third, we know, too, how a statement can be distorted in transmission. Many of us as children played the classroom game in which the teacher started a sentence around the room by whispering it to one child, he to the next, and so on, until, after forty children had passed on the sentence, it came out quite altered from the mouth of the last child.

What has religion to say to all this? The more orthodox churchmen are generally inhospitable to such interpretations, particularly to the suggestion that the event described never took place. Nor are they too sympathetic to the view that, while something did take place, it was imperfectly understood or elaborated in transmission or both. Yet there are others within the camp of religion who do not react quite so strongly. They may not go so far as to say that the events described never took place, but they are willing to grant that they were imperfectly understood at the time and perhaps elaborated in the process of transmission.

For example, an explanation has been suggested for the Biblical account of Moses and the children of Israel passing through the waters of the Red Sea in their escape from Egypt. This is that Moses knew just where and when the waters of the Red Sea would be at their lowest level and managed to effect the crossing at that particular time and place. It has even been suggested that he took into account the shifting of the winds, which were instrumental in separating the waters.

So too with the tumbling of the walls of Jericho, to mention just one more example. You will remember that when the Hebrews attacked Jericho, their point of entry into the Promised Land, they were told to "compass the city seven times," blowing horns while they marched around the city. At a final, long blast of the ram's horns, all the people were to "shout with a great shout" and the walls of the city would fall. It has been suggested that sound, of the proper pitch and intensity, might account for the collapse of the walls of Jericho, in the same way that sound can shatter glass.

There may indeed be some validity in this type of reasoning. While from the viewpoint of the liberal religionist all of the Biblical references need not be taken literally, we must be nonetheless aware that archaeological researches in the areas covered by the Bible narrative have come up with some rather fascinating discoveries validating a number of these Biblical records.

In the story of the destruction of Sodom and Gomorrah, for example, there is a reference to "brimstone and fire from the Lord out of heaven" consuming these cities. Interpreting this fire as indicating the presence of natural gas, and on the premise that where there is natural gas there is likely to be oil, a company was organized recently in Israel which found geological evidence of the presence of oil at that site.

Again, in the first book of Kings, we are told that Solomon's copper mines were located in Ezion-geber, "beside Elath, on the shore of the Red Sea in the land of Edom." Dr. Nelson Glueck, the archaeologist, explored the area and actually found those mines. These experiences indicate that we should not cavalierly dismiss Biblical references as fantasy.

But this does not fully confront the problem of miracles in the Bible. For some of the miracles described in it are not easily explained and therefore remain miracles, to be accepted or rejected as such. These references do seem to run counter to the laws of nature as we understand them. How are we to explain Elijah's ascent into heaven in a chariot of fire? Or how explain the transformation of the staff of Moses into a serpent? These seem to defy all attempts to "explain" them. Thus the religious liberal takes the view that these are examples of hyperbole, that they represent poeticized versions of reality.

When Homer, in the *Odyssey,* spoke of "the rosy-fingered dawn," he certainly did not mean that the dawn had rosy fingers. And when Carl Sandburg spoke of the fog coming in on "little cat feet," he surely did not mean that this was to be taken literally. So it may be that some of these miracles are poeticized or dramatized interpretations of events in history.

It should be remembered, of course, that this material was not written in the twentieth century, as the record of a scientific observer, but many centuries ago, by men who used poetic imagery rather than scientific language; that they were unashamedly partisan in the account they were unfolding, with none of the detachment of the scientist, and employed the richly symbolic language of the ancient Orient.

Such literary material invariably grows up about the life of a great personality, or about a significant event in the history of a people. It is only a century and a half since the time of George Washington, yet we already have the story of his chopping down the cherry tree, and of his throwing a silver dollar across the Potomac. (Some wit has explained the latter by saying that the dollar went farther in those days.) In similar fashion, a number of stories cluster about the personality of Abraham Lincoln, though it is less than a century since he died.

Is it then to be wondered at that the Hebrews of long ago, describing the greatest event in their history, the exodus from Egypt which started them on the long road through history, told of awesome plagues that came upon the Egyptians before the Hebrews were set free? That which we cherish, we embellish. The diamond is given a setting of black velvet to reveal its beauty to the utmost. It is made into a ring for the finger of a loved one because we cherish her. How much more do the great events in the history of a people lend themselves to artistic adornment!

What then shall we say about miracles? Just this: the critically minded cannot accept the idea that the laws of nature were at any time suspended. That would be an affront to science. It may be, however, that some things have happened in this world which are miracles, in the dictionary sense that they "deviate from the known laws of nature, or transcend our knowledge of these laws," so that our knowledge of the laws of nature will have to expand before we can cease to call them miracles.

But it may also be true that some of these miracles are a fine lace, spun by the human heart, in tribute to the things it loves. And from the viewpoint of the liberal religionist, religion need not depend on miracle; it need not stand or fall by it. For more marvelous than the suspension of natural law is its continuous operation. And more important than miracle is religion itself. The yearning of man for the infinite is by far the greater "miracle."

The Sense of Sin

In the Bible, evil is regarded as sin; not as an affront to the standards of society, but to the demands of divinity.

Men familiar with Scripture and steeped in its spirit have often differed as to what constitutes sin, but that right and wrong can be defined, that right thought and action are required of us, and that these are in keeping with God's plan, have rarely been doubted. And, in the formulation of a mature religious faith, we cannot escape the confrontation of this concept.

For a brief time, just a generation ago, we seemed to be on the verge of "emancipation" from such thinking. Some of us remember the late twenties, when relativism in morality was the vogue, when many men and women were no longer convinced that there was such a thing as sin. Judge Ben Lindsey championed the cause of companionate marriage, behind which was the notion that the only way to find out whether a marriage would work was to try it for a while and see. There was no thought given to the responsibility of the two contracting parties to *make* the marriage work.

The mood of the period was expressed by Mrs. Bertrand Russell who declared, "Animals are we, and animals we remain, and the road to our happiness, if there be such a road, lies through our animal nature." Men even joked about sin, telling the story of Calvin Coolidge, a notably taciturn man, who upon his return from church one Sunday was asked by his wife what the preacher had talked about. "Sin," said Silent Cal. And when his wife asked, "But what did he say about it?" Coolidge replied, "He was against it."

The *zeitgeist*—the spirit of the times—was one of new freedom, of abandonment of "outgrown" restraints, indeed of religion itself. And in such an atmosphere the idea of sin could only be regarded as old-fashioned. Not that men abandoned all principles of personal morality—they didn't; but they thought it absurd to ascribe religious sanctions to a relativistic morality which they felt must emerge, if at all, from the fields of sociology and anthropology, investigating the habits of the Bantus and Polynesians as well as our own.

The *zeitgeist* of yesteryear, however, is not that of today. Theology has now gained a new respectability and enjoys a prestige it has not held for some time. And one of the chief concerns of contemporary theologians is the concept of sin. It has become the focus of thought for such men as Reinhold Niebuhr and Karl Barth, in the New World and in the Old. The sinfulness of man has been construed as the cause of individual discontent and social disharmony. The story of Cain and Abel, in line with an older theology, is increasingly read as the story of man's sinful nature. It is being stretched to universal scale, to explain the two world wars we have witnessed, the savagery of Nazism, the atomic destruction of Hiroshima. We have become recently aware of man's capacity for organized brutality, and we have, as a consequence, reverted from the mood of a generation ago to the earlier emphasis upon the reality of sin.

The re-recognition of sin is not to be taken lightly. We dare not minimize the moral debacle we have witnessed in our time. We ought never to forget the Nazi doctors—men of science, engaged purely in research—who submerged living persons in water, gradually reducing the temperature, to determine at what point the human heart would stop beating. We have seen the fierceness of man—unguided by a sense of sin, undisturbed by feelings of guilt—acting without conscience or compassion. Our optimism about man's ability to handle his problems rationally and humanely has been shaken.

In view of recent history, we cannot, in attempting to achieve religious maturity, dismiss the term "sin" as outmoded theological cant. It serves to describe an area of human behavior and responsibility that no other term can properly do. Sin is more than "error"; it is more than "making a mistake." When you add two and two and get five, you have made an error. When you've taken a wrong turn on the highway, you've made a mistake. In the first instance carelessness, in the second lack of proper information, is to blame. In both, the error is easily rectified, and no one is likely to be hurt.

But this is not true when men are put to death in crematories or blown to bits by an atomic explosion. Not when you have broken the Ten Commandments. Not when you've injured another person, his family, his livelihood, his reputation, or even his feelings. If we regard human life and personality as inviolable, these things are sins. Robbing, cheating, or slandering another is a sin. Insulting, shaming, or embarrassing another is a sin. It is an affront to God, the Author of life and of its capacity for growth and fulfillment, both in terms of what it does to the offended and what it does to the offender. It is a diminution of the divinity in each.

To be sure, there are gradations of sin. Embarrassing another is not on a plane with adultery; insulting another is not on a plane with murder. If, as some religious groups hold, sin is prompted by the devil, are not some sins more "diabolical" than others? While temptations to sin may surround us, all are not equal giants. Yet religion is right in reminding us that even the lesser ones must be overcome, for the conquest of the lesser may encourage and strengthen us for the conquest of the greater. Having conquered the sin of slander, we can more easily conquer the sin of murder, for we have already "conquered" ourselves.

Yet the sin-dominated theology of an earlier day, of "O, what a worm am I," ought not to be resurrected uncritically with the "rediscovery" of sin. We have learned not to underestimate man's capacity for sin, but we must also be careful not to exaggerate it. We must somehow steer a course between the all-pervasive consciousness of sin of an earlier era and the radical ridicule of it that prevailed a generation ago.

The very Scriptures which describe the sinfulness of man also depict his spirituality. Cain is not altogether the prototype of man; Amos is, and Isaiah is, and so are the other great prophets. Or rather, all of them together are, for each presents an aspect of the human potential for good and evil. Man is not altogether sinful nor altogether sinless. Jesus recognized that fact when he challenged the man without guilt to cast the first stone at the adulterous woman.

The profligate Sidney Carton in Dickens' *A Tale of Two Cities* was capable of sacrificing himself on the guillotine in place of another, for the happiness of the woman he loved. Conversely, the minister in Somerset Maugham's *Rain*, despite his religious training and fervor, capitulated to the charms of the wanton woman he set out to save. This admixture of strength and weakness, good and evil, is not to be found in fiction alone. It exists all around us and in the personality portraits of the very heroes of our faith: in Joseph, the spoiled and self-centered brat, reconciled at last with his brothers in love; in Peter, who thrice denied Jesus, yet became "the rock" upon which the church was built.

It is not true, as is sometimes alleged, that priestcraft is responsible for imbuing men with a sense of sin and exploiting their guilt-feelings to its own advantage. The consciousness of sin is somehow reflexive—a sense of disruption of inner harmony, a loss of self-respect, an alienation from God, which men often experience without benefit of clergy. It is part of the mechanism of conscience itself. Religion did not *invent* sin; it *discovered* sin and discovered its impact upon the sinner as well as on the sinned-against. It has sought to meliorate the sense of guilt and to channelize it creatively, helping men not only to express, through confession and atonement, the wrongs they committed, but also to redirect their lives.

The achievement of a sane view of sin, involving neither the repudiation of its existence nor the exaggeration of its hold on us, is necessary to our proper acceptance of others and to our proper acceptance of ourselves. We can refrain from merciless condemnation, from a "holier-than-thou" attitude toward others. And if we are the sinners, we can refrain from neurotic, exaggerated feelings of guilt, saving ourselves needless torture and utilizing that same psychic energy for setting ourselves new directions and disciplining ourselves to follow them. The answer to our feelings of guilt is not the denial of the existence of sin but the repudiation of sin itself. "Cease to do evil, learn to do good," is the simple way that Isaiah expressed it. He recognized that our creative and compassionate impulses must be rescued from the morass of our destructive urges. This involves not self-castigation but the recovery of self-esteem, the achievement of rapport not only with man and God but with ourselves.

Of Law and Love

Much of the material in the early books of the Bible, particularly in Exodus and Leviticus, is legalistic. The moral law is rendered specific in a body of legislation, in a series of Thou Shalts and Thou Shalt Nots. One is struck by the number and variety not only of the laws themselves but also of the very terms used for them: "Ye shall walk in my *statutes*"; " . . . and keep my *commandments*"; "Now these are the *ordinances*"; "This is the *law*."

In Exodus we find not only the Ten Commandments but also ordinances dealing with the treatment of slaves, with murder, kidnaping, and bodily injury. There too we find laws governing sex relations, laws forbidding idolatry, and the cryptic injunction not to "seethe a kid in its mother's milk." And it is there that we read "eye for eye, tooth for tooth, hand for hand, foot for foot, burning for burning, stripe for stripe."

The statute, "eye for eye, tooth for tooth," is sometimes cited to indicate that Old Testament law is rigid and remorseless—although in capital punishment our "enlightened" society still practices it. Actually, it served to replace an older morality of unlimited retribution. Before then, if one put out the eye of another, he, or even his whole family, might be vengefully put to death. Under the new principle the punishment of a criminal had to "fit the crime," was to be commensurate with the crime, and was not to exceed it. Seen in this light, the eighteenth century practice of hanging men for theft was far more primitive than "eye for eye" and "tooth for tooth."

Nonetheless, there are those who feel that the Old Testament is unduly legalistic, and contrast is occasionally drawn between the Old Testament and the New, the one being said to embody the spirit of law, the other the spirit of love. But is even that really true? Hebraic legislation covers permissible and forbidden foods, even permissible and forbidden clothing, as well as interpersonal relations, in the attempt to establish a total pattern of life. Thus Leviticus sets forth the regulations for the temple priests in conducting their ritual, and we are told about the bullocks, the heifers, and doves that are to be brought as sacrifices: we are told about the heave-offerings and the wave-offerings. Yet imbedded in the very midst of the most technical sacrificial jargon we find the magnificent statement, "Ye shall be holy, for I the Lord your God am holy." It is in this very sequence of material that we read, "And thou shalt love thy neighbor as thyself." The whole body of law is geared to the goal of man's moral perfection.

While the Old Testament emphasis on law is real, its separation from love is not. The note of compassion runs strong. Indeed, in the book of Proverbs, we read, "Rejoice not when thine enemy falleth, And let not thine heart be glad when he stumbleth." It is in the same book that we read, "If thine enemy be hungry, give him bread to eat, And if thine enemy thirsteth, give him water to drink." How strikingly reminiscent of the New Testament admonition that we love our enemies! Surely the idea of loving our enemies was not altogether new, or was but a step beyond the feeling here expressed.

For the prophets, so much concerned with social righteousness, love is translated into justice. Their call is specific and clear: they refer to the poor, the widow and orphan, the "stranger in the gates," and the laborer. They speak up for "just balances, just weights," and for the sacredness of the pledged word.

But justice finds expression in law; justice is the bond between love and law. Love leads to justice and justice to law. Without law there will be not love but anarchy, as each man does what is right in his own eyes. The fulfillment of the requirements of morality—the requirements of love—is not left to chance, nor is it left entirely to the good intentions men profess. The prophets are bolstered and supported by the law, by ordinances *protecting* the poor, the widow, and the orphan: "Thou shalt not oppress the widow and the fatherless"; *safeguarding* the rights of the alien: "the stranger shall be unto you as the home born"; by legislation *upholding* the rights of the workingman: "Thou shalt not keep the wages of a hired man overnight."

Does the varying emphasis on law and love mark a real distinction between Judaism and Christianity? Much has recently been written about the Dead Sea Scrolls and about that group of Jews who lived in the Qumran caves where these were found. Among the documents discovered was the Manual of Discipline, which sheds a good deal of light on what these people thought and how they lived. While there are differences, one is struck by the similarities of thought and practice found in this Jewish monastic community and among the early Christians. And we are rather sharply reminded that the emergence of Christianity out of Judaic sources was not really a sharp break, was as much evolutionary as it was revolutionary.

The same holds true for the distinction between love and law in the two faiths. While the emphasis in each may differ, it would be as wrong to say that love is not found in the Old Testament as that law is not found in the New. Certainly in the writings of Paul attempts are made to formulate Christian thought and practice. And Jesus himself is quoted as saying that he came "not to abrogate the law but to fulfill it."

The exact degree to which law is emphasized in the Old Testament and love in the New is, however, of academic interest only. It is more important to recognize the relevance of each and its relationship to the other.

Law represents love in action. The feeling for others cannot remain purely nebulous. Where it is genuine, it will be applied to life situations. (All of us have probably met persons who "love mankind" in the abstract yet have little love for *people*.) The man who loves his neighbor will not rob or cheat him; the man who loves his family will not desert it but will provide for it. Nonetheless we have laws to prevent us from robbing or cheating our neighbors, and we have laws to restrain us from abandoning our families!

Some laws can and do become obsolete. There are statutes on the books of our cities and states that are no longer meaningful. Now and then a newspaper feature lists some of these ordinances, and we chuckle at the changes time has brought. There are regulations that a horse left unattended on the street must be tethered, that pumps for drinking water must be regularly inspected, though we now drive cars instead of carriages and draw our drinking-water from the tap in the kitchen sink.

These statutes are rarely repealed but generally ignored, for they are no longer vital, no longer relevant to our lives. But we neither repeal nor ignore the laws against murder, theft, and arson. And we do not, even in repudiating outmoded legislation, repudiate the need for law. Indeed, the likelihood is that every law that has been rendered obsolete will be replaced by several others, to meet the even more complex conditions of our day.

To be sure, Biblical law is presented as divine legislation, and we should be reluctant to treat it lightly. Yet we ought to recognize that the moral law in the Bible, together with its specific statutes and ordinances, represents the attempt to achieve the good life and the good society in keeping with a much earlier pattern of civilization, one far different from our own. How, for example, are we to regard the Biblical injunction, "Thou shalt not suffer a witch to live," or the prohibition against wearing garments made of a mixture of wool and linen? Are these to be put on the same level with the Ten Commandments, or with the injunction that we feed our enemies and love our neighbors?

Just as we may make the mistake of worshipping the Bible instead of God (the error of Bibliolatry), so must we be careful not to reverence the letter of its law more than the spirit behind it. Law is subject to interpretation. The Supreme Court is constantly being called upon to interpret the Constitution, written nearly two centuries ago in a largely agrarian setting, for a new industrial civilization. Mosaic law too has been interpreted by the Jews through the ages, and we ought to apply our best insights and information to that Biblical legislation, to determine how, or to what extent, it is to govern our lives.

We must give heed not only to its *interpretation,* but also to its *motivation.* For if law requires proper interpretation, it requires proper motivation as well. Often in the Biblical legislation we are made to fear the consequence of non-compliance with threats of punishment. In other instances we are asked to obey so that "your lives may be lengthened in the land which the Lord your God giveth you," or that we may be blessed with abundance. But neither fear of punishment nor hope of reward is mature motivation for morality. Indeed, such motivations for morality can themselves be immoral, imposing repressive fear or arousing selfish aims. And Biblical legislation itself outgrows these motivations. Is not the charge, "Ye shall be holy, *for I the Lord your God am holy,"* much more exalted?

In the attempt to achieve a mature religious philosophy, the Biblical code of morality cannot be ignored. The Ten Commandments are certainly vital; so is the injunction that we love our neighbors, and so is a good deal more. We might, for example, benefit by a review of the specific ordinances dealing with sex morality in this day of Kinsey reports and confused sex standards. We might benefit from the text and spirit of the Mosaic morality in developing a body of international law, a vast new need in the shrunken world of our day where all men are "neighbors."

Much of the Biblical morality *is* divine law, in the sense that it is universally and eternally applicable, that noble individual living and the good society are impossible without it. The breaking of that law is, in the deepest sense, a sin. And we are challenged, individually and collectively, to rediscover and reassess that law, to give it meaningful expression in our interpersonal and international dealings. Law need not be an obstacle to love; it is through law that love is often best expressed, and the love of law can serve as a tremendous force in the fulfillment of the law of love.

Priest, Prophet, and Psalmist

The Bible, as a compilation of religious writings covering a thousand years of time, reveals various conceptions of God. Some of the references to divinity, such as God's walking in the Garden of Eden, may seem somewhat primitive to us. Others, however, like the reference to God as "the still small voice" within ourselves, are no less than sublime.

Basically, the Bible contains three approaches to God: those of the priest, the prophet, and the psalmist. Of the three, the approach of the priest is the oldest and most limited. Its emphasis is on ritual acts, on custom and accoutrements, on externals. But the priestly form of worship is not the highest achievement in the Biblical development of religion. The approach of the prophet and that of the psalmist represent a considerable advance.

That advance is part of the remarkable story of the development of religion itself. In early forms of religion, man—so dependent on the things around him—first discerns divinity *in* these *things*: in rocks and stones, in the trees of the forest, in the rivers and streams. Each thing has its own spirit. If one wants to cut down a tree, one must first ask forgiveness of the tree spirit. If one would safely cross a stream, one must first address himself to the river spirit. In early conceptions of religion, all things are animated, each thing possessing—or possessed by—its own spirit.

The earliest forms of religious worship and ritual similarly involve *things*. The medicine man wears a mask, paints his face, and ornaments his body. He wears a special garb as he intercedes with the gods on behalf of his people or of a sick individual. He goes through an elaborate rite, in which *things* are involved. Often that ritual is symbolic of the nature of his petition. In his prayer for rain, water is poured from a pitcher. In praying for the conquest of an enemy, a pin is thrust into a figurine made to resemble that enemy.

But something happens in the growth of religion which is perhaps akin to what happens in the growth of the individual. There is movement from the concrete to the abstract and from the particular to the universal. A child knows what a toothache is before he understands the concept of pain; he knows what an apple is before he understands the concept of fruit. So it is with the growth of religion. Vague conceptions of divinity in natural objects yield to the belief in certain fixed tribal gods. Finally, these tribal gods coalesce and, no longer associated with the soil of any land or the soul of any people, become one God, the God of all nature and of all mankind.

Advance in religious thinking is somewhat similar to advance in scientific thinking: in both cases the law of parsimony operates. In science, we seek a single answer for a multitude of phenomena, where a multitude of answers have previously been given. We find an explanation of the way in which one object falls to the ground, and abstract from it a principle to describe how all objects fall, how the very stars and planets act upon each other. So too in religious thinking. We move, as in science, from many explanations to one. We move from many meanings to one meaning, from a fragmentized universe to an integrated universe. Ultimately we move from a fragmentized humanity to an integrated humanity, from a fragmented individual to a unified man.

Something of this development from the concrete to the abstract, from the particular to the universal, that is characteristic of the growth of religion is revealed to us in the Bible.

The priestly ritual represents rather strikingly a formalistic, externalized approach to religion. *Things*—and the way they were handled—were important. God demanded sacrifices: a bull for certain occasions, a dove or lamb for still other occasions. The animals selected had to meet certain specifications. These sacrifices were to be offered up in conformity with a fixed ceremony. Certain parts of the animal were to be burned; other parts were to be treated differently.

But even while the Temple stood, with all of its rich panoply of punctilious procedure, the prophets appeared upon the scene. Indeed, the Temple ritual was to continue for centuries after they made their appearance. Yet these spiritual giants of human history discovered and taught a different approach to religion. They discovered God in human relationships.

They felt that men were somehow divinely related to one another, that they were brothers and must treat one another as such. The prophet Amos cried out, "Let justice well up as waters, and righteousness as a mighty stream." The prophet Hosea spoke of love. And Isaiah envisioned a world at peace. They tried to translate the unity they discerned in the universe into the unity of mankind. What was the sacrifice that God demanded? Not burnt-offerings, declared the prophets, but "to clothe the naked, to feed the hungry, to care for the poor, the widow and the orphan."

The prophets were mighty exponents of the idea that all mankind is one, that each of us is indeed his brother's keeper, that man and man, nation and nation, are responsibly bound to one another. Thus they were impelled to declare that injustice must cease, that war must be eliminated. They contributed to the religion of the Hebrews and to the advance of religion generally a lofty, ethical drive, which was either absent or obscured until their time.

The birds or beasts brought to the Temple for sacrifice were minutely examined by the priests to determine whether they were disqualified by any blemish. Yet the character of the man who brought that sacrifice was not subjected to similar scrutiny. It was the prophets who exhorted men to examine their own hearts and to act in accordance with their inmost conscience.

But even the prophet does not represent the peak of religious development in the pages of the Bible. While religion grew beyond rigid ritual to social awareness in the thunderings of the prophets, it achieved its highest inwardness in the anguished utterances of the psalmist. He recognized the unity and grandeur of the universe; indeed, he described it magnificently. He recognized too the relatedness of the human family and his own place in it. But he also looked *within* himself.

He sought the meaning of his own existence, the meaning of his own discomfitures, his own triumphs, the goals of his own living. He recognized his faults and expressed his penitence; he knew his weakness and sought God's strength. The prophets proclaimed the relevance of God to human society; the psalmist discovered the relevance of God to the individual— and of the individual to God. "The Lord is my shepherd, I shall not want" is his superb declaration of faith. "Like as a father hath pity upon his children, so doth the Lord have pity upon me" is his statement of trust. He expresses man's personal relationship with the infinite, his irrepressible urge for linkage with the divine. "As the deer panteth after the water-brook, so doth my soul thirst for Thee."

Man longing for God! The individual thirsting for divinity! Here is religion stripped of all externals, here is religion completely personalized, completely inwardized. The psalmist has done more than relate himself to his fellow man;

he has done more than relate himself to nature. He has related himself to the very spirit that animates both.

> Whither shall I flee from Thy spirit,
> Or whither escape from Thy presence?
> If I mount into heaven, Thou art there;
> If I make my bed in the netherworld,
> Behold, Thou art there.
> If I take the wings of the morning,
> And dwell in the uttermost parts of the sea,
> Even there would Thy hand lead me,
> And Thy right hand would hold me.

The priest represents religion in terms of *form,* in terms of externals. The prophet represents religion in terms of *function,* in terms of brotherhood and peace. The psalmist represents religion in terms of *faith,* in terms of his discovery of God and God's discovery of him.

While the faith of the psalmist might seem to be the highest achievement in religion, the function of religion in the world of men, as represented by the prophet, and the form of religion, as represented by the priest, are not really superseded, are not necessarily displaced. As we achieve religious maturity, we move from form to function to faith and then move back again. For, having achieved faith, we will want to give it function, in our social outlook and relationships; and we will want to give it form in our mode of worship.

The faith we possess, once personalized and inwardized, must still be socialized and humanized, must move outward to embrace mankind; it must yet be dramatized and verbalized through ritual and prayer. For faith may be sterile and barren without function or form. The challenge to the maturely religious is to give it such meaningful function and form as to render that faith creative in our own lives and in the lives of others.

4

FORGING THE FUTURE

The Insights of Psychiatry

The field of psychiatry has opened new vistas for the understanding of human behavior. It has provided us with a whole new set of concepts and a new terminology, which have become part of our language and way of life.

Almost daily we are likely to hear someone speak of frustrations and repressions, of conflicts and aggressions, or to use these terms ourselves. If a woman is inclined to eat a full pound of chocolates at one sitting, we are likely to describe that as a form of compensation. If a man strikes his son upon returning home from a hard day at work, we are likely to think of that action as a displaced aggression—he can't strike his boss, so strikes his son instead.

Yet we are apt to be somewhat ambivalent about our acceptance of psychiatry, to accept it just a bit grudgingly. Probably the most common type of joke in our day is the psychiatrist story. There is one which tells of the psychiatrist who cured a little boy of an unusual attachment to his hobby-horse by merely whispering something into his ear. The child immediately jumped off the horse, and the astonished parents asked the doctor what he had said to the youngster. The psychiatrist replied, "I told him that if he didn't get off that hobby-horse I'd break his neck."

The very fact that there are so many "psychiatrist

stories" is an indication of the impact of psychiatry in our day. Most of us are aware of the importance of psychiatric insights and the opportunities they offer for a better understanding of the deeper levels of human personality, motivation, and behavior.

Yet the forces of traditional religion have been slow to admit that psychiatry *has* new insights to offer. Traditional religion has generally found itself at war with psychiatry, finding it in conflict with religious doctrine. The traditional religionist objects that psychiatry holds a non-theological view of sin and thereby eliminates the need for confession and atonement. He objects that psychiatry tries to rid man of his sense of guilt, which he believes necessary for man's sense of moral responsibility.

Psychiatry, for its part, has not been too friendly toward traditional religion. Psychiatry has tended to regard God as a crutch for dependent personalities and as a projection of the father image. Belief in God has thus been regarded as evidence of immaturity, of unwillingness to grow up. Indeed, psychiatry has been inclined to regard all of religion as a "mass neurosis" into which the individual escapes to save himself from falling into a neurosis of his own under the pressures and tensions of life.

There are, to be sure, some basic differences between religion—certainly the more conservative religions—and psychiatry. But actually, this conflict between psychiatry and religion is more theoretical than real; more on the conceptual level than on the level of action. Each has demonstrated that it has a function to perform in helping the individual. Each has made a real contribution to an understanding of the conflicts that arise between person and person, group and group, as well as within the individual. And there is the growing feeling that each can be of considerable service to the other.

The battle for the soul of man—if psychiatrists will accept the term—still rages between the extremists in the camps of both psychiatry and religion. But the forces of reconciliation are stronger and are gaining ground steadily. Some of the large city churches and temples engage psychiatrists to aid the clergy in their pastoral function. Indeed, more and more clergymen are sending their parishioners to psychiatrists, while more and more psychiatrists are sending their patients to church! At the Hebrew Union College, in Cincinnati, where Reform rabbis are trained, special lectures are given relating psychiatry and religion. And at the Union Theological Seminary in New York, where Protestant ministers are trained, there is now a full-time Professor of Psychiatry on the teaching staff.

In view of the seemingly vast theoretical gap between psychiatry and religion, isn't this a rather strange turn of events? Why then has this happened? It is because the practitioners of both psychiatry and religion have undergone some maturation, some "mellowing." Both have begun to recognize that each may have something to gain from the experiences and insights of the other.

Psychiatrists today, dealing with their patients' inner difficulties, are beginning to recognize that they can learn something from the ministrations of church and synagogue. Working with the individual up until now as a detached personality, they are now more aware that men want to feel at home in the universe. Men want to feel that the world of nature is not a hostile, nor even an indifferent, place but a friendly place. And it has been one of the basic functions of religion to give man the feeling of being "at home" in the world around him.

Again, they are beginning to recognize that even enlightened men and women—indeed, particularly the enlightened, who so often break down in the effort to find their own way—need some rules and patterns for the conduct of life, for living their lives with others. Men need some scale of values to render life meaningful. Religion, through its moral precepts, has consistently given men such guidance, teaching them how best to live in and with the world of men.

Above all, psychiatrists are learning from the ministrations of religion that men are likely to experience their deepest difficulties if they have lost the very mainspring of life—faith. Without faith in the worthwhileness of life, there can be no faith in the worthwhileness of oneself; and without such faith, life itself becomes a nightmare. Dr. C. G. Jung, whom Freud once acclaimed as his successor, has said:

> As a doctor, I have had experience with thousands of people from all parts of the world, who have told me the stories of their lives, their hopes, their fears. . . . As a result, I have become convinced that the problem of today is a religious problem. Man needs the sustaining influence of religious faith more today than ever before; otherwise, the quickened tempo of modern life and the complexity of modern civilization will thrust upon men neurasthenias and psychoses disastrous to the life of the individual.

Religion has been the reservoir of faith through the ages, and with faith it still strengthens men in moments of crisis and decision, to meet the challenge of living.

If psychiatry has all this to learn from religion, religion as well can learn much from psychiatry. Between psychiatry and religion there is a "two-way passage." Religion, in its concern with the morality of men, can learn a great deal from psychiatry about the motivations of human behavior, about the causes of much of our conduct. Religion should certainly be interested in the reasons *why* men do the things they do, or fail to do the things they *ought* to do, if it is to be really successful in directing human behavior into constructive, moral channels. Now that psychiatry has given us greater insight into why we behave—or misbehave—like human be-

ings, ministers equipped with these insights are better able to
understand the people they are working with, thus better able
to help them.

Religion at its highest has taught us not to blame nor to
hate. The insights of psychiatry now support and confirm
these teachings. The boy who has been caught stealing may
be in need of healing rather than in need of punishment, in
need of love. He may be the product of problem parents. The
man who has wronged his neighbor may be in need of understanding rather than blame. He may be a troubled individual
who is finding an outlet for hostility. And much the same
thing is true for the nations of the world. If religion teaches
us not to blame, nor to hate, psychiatry helps show us why—
what insecurities, immaturities, and conflicts are involved,
both in the person casting blame and in the one upon whom
it is cast. The ethics of religion become more significant and
compelling in the light of psychiatric considerations.

The newspapers reported some time ago the story of a
Chicago millionaire who was emotionally disturbed and seeing a psychiatrist. The psychiatrist found that the man was
too absorbed in himself, that he had no responsibilities, no
real interests to capture his attention. He advised the patient
to establish a philanthropic foundation to systematically dis-
pose of some of his millions and to supervise the work per-
sonally. The patient did just that and became so engrossed in
the work of evaluating the applications for funds and adjust-
ing the disbursements to the needs of the applicants that he
became a changed individual. He did not need psychiatric
treatment much longer. Good psychiatry? Yes, but good
religion too!

Theoretically, psychiatry and religion are poles apart.
Psychiatry is interested in producing a happy man, an integrated man, or, to use still another term, a mature man; it is
interested in the achievement, too, of a "sane" society. Religion is classically concerned with producing a moral man, a

good man; and with producing the "good" society. But religion and psychiatry are not really aiming in two different directions, but in the same direction. For the good man is more likely to be the integrated or mature man, while the integrated or mature man is more likely to be the good man. And the "good" society is likely to be the "sane" society.

Does this sound strange? It isn't, really. A man disturbed by inner conflicts is not a happy man, nor is he likely to be a truly good man. Scrooge, in Dickens' *Christmas Carol*, could not be good because he was unhappy. Even if the unhappy man makes the effort to be good, his very "goodness" is apt to be unwholesome, to be exaggerated, reflecting an exaggerated need for acceptance. One cannot be at peace with others until he is at peace with himself. One cannot properly integrate himself with others until he has integrated himself.

Psychiatry seeks to *free* the individual, while religion seeks to *transform* him. Yet love is the key to both. From the standpoint of psychiatry, the ability to love is the test of maturity; from the standpoint of religion the expression of love is the best of morality. Psychiatry seeks to release love, and religion seeks to implement it. But psychiatry and religion both recognize the paramount importance of love, and from this agreement they can work together to make man whole, at one with himself and with those around him.

Family Harmony

The character of the American home is variously assessed by current observers. Some depict it as a TV-centered place where there is very little personal interplay, a place where one changes his clothes to go somewhere else. Others note that there is a new sense of family solidarity emerging in American life—that we are becoming a home-building and home-loving nation.

Whether or not we are making of our homes vital

centers of character growth, our generation is fortunate to have at its disposal psychological insights which can help us in that objective. Better understanding of our children, and of parent-child relationships, is readily available through paperback books, talks on radio and TV, magazine articles, and newspaper columns, which provide us with abundant guidance in these areas of family living.

But I am reminded of the cartoon in which two children are playing in the gutter and one of them, looking up and seeing his mother approaching, says, "Let's get out of here. There comes mother with that child-psychology look in her eye."

I wonder whether we do not go about the business too self-consciously and try a little too hard—whether we are not sometimes even guilty of following the "party line." Take the matter of self-expression. Not so long ago it was perfectly permissible for Junior to use a hammer on the piano keys. "Nothing must be done to frustrate the child" was the prevailing dictum. Now it is more popular to believe that "a little frustration is a good thing; it prepares the child for the inevitable frustrations that lie ahead."

Perhaps we are somewhat *over*-reliant on "child psychology." This dependence on what the experts say betrays our own uncertainties and confusions, our absence of genuine personal standards and strong convictions as to what is good and bad, right and wrong—perhaps an inevitable consequence of the social changes we are living through.

Yet today's parents are *seeking* guidance, not spurning it. Theirs is the grace of humility and the sincere desire to *be* more competent parents: to *gain* better understanding in the area of family relationships, and to *achieve* a set of values to transmit to their children.

This is where psychological insights and the teachings of religion can be helpful—where these two disciplines, complementing each other, may serve to strengthen the home and develop the character of our children. For psychological understanding of the child in itself is inadequate: we are still called upon to provide the child with *spiritual values*, values to live by, in his relationships with himself and others. Conversely, religious principles cannot properly be taught in the home in defiance of psychological truths: we must know the nature of the child and his needs in order to teach these principles effectively.

Religion in the home usually involves some form of prayer. Yet the nature of that prayer is important. It must be related to the experience of the individual to be meaningful; it must be a source of strength to be fruitful in his life. Certainly this cannot be said for the old night prayer for children, "Now I lay me down to sleep / I pray the Lord my soul to keep / And if I die before I wake / I pray the Lord my soul to take."

To be sure, this is an obviously horrible example. Yet we ought to ask, in connection with prayer in the home, Is it related to the child's experience, therefore meaningful to him? Will it help him in facing life? Does it build courage, unselfishness, co-operation, or does it implant in his mind denigrating conceptions of himself and distorted conceptions of divinity, which he will later have to outgrow, perhaps with traumatic consequences? We might go further and ask: Does that prayer do anything at all for the child? I am thinking of the youngster who in his night prayers asked God to bless his dog, his cat, and almost everything he could think of—simply to forestall going to sleep.

We ordinarily assume that home Bible reading is good. And of course it can be, if properly approached. But so can the stories of George Washington, Abraham Lincoln, and Jane Addams, while some of the Bible stories do anything but stir moral or pious urges in young readers or listeners. What mixed response must be produced in a child listening to the story of the "sacrifice" of Isaac! Though the Psalms are sublime religious poetry, what do they mean to a young-ster? One is reminded of the child who had learned the Twenty-third Psalm at Sunday School and spoke of "Good Miss Murphy" who would "follow me all the days of my life."

To be sure, prayer, Bible reading, and other forms of religious expression in the home have their value. On the lowest level, they help to create a sense of order and pattern in the home and contribute by their immutability of wording and regularity of recurrence a feeling-tone of security which is a good bulwark against the daily uncertainties of life. Yet religion in the home ought to do more than that. It should link us with the good, the true, and the beautiful—with the eternal and unchanging. It should heighten our aspirations and stretch our souls.

We can allow our zeal to outstrip our wisdom in the attempt to create a religious home atmosphere. We may indeed feed the uncertainty and anxiety which it is intended to allay. The father of Elizabeth Barrett Browning was a "religious" man, yet he wrought incalculable harm in the development of his children's character. The "fear of God" he taught them was personified in their fear of their father; neither was good for their personal growth. Mr. Barrett's "religion" was authoritative and unyielding, with little room for understanding and tenderness.

More important than formal religious *acts* in furthering the religious life of the family are religious *attitudes*. We should address ourselves primarily to creating those attitudes of self-regard and regard for others, of confidence, courage, and generosity, of unselfishness and honesty, which form the very essence of a healthy religious life.

The paraphernalia of prayer, Bible reading, and cere-monialism may and ought to be adjuncts and instruments toward the creation of a religious atmosphere, to verbalize and dramatize the values we seek to transmit. If these values are given appropriate expression in religious terminology and ceremony, they may thereby be further reinforced. But only if these are truly meaningful to the parent.

Any father who, himself fearing dogs, has held a child's hand and told him not to be afraid when a dog happened along, knows how little his words alone will mean to the child. Within the family circle—as in all of our relationships—what we say is not nearly as important as what we do; and what we do is not nearly so important as what we are and the way we feel. The mood that we generate is what really counts.

Mildred and Frank Eakin, in *Your Child's Religion*, note that even in the stress of depression and war children respond less to outer circumstances than to their parents' reactions to these situations. They found that where the parents responded to emergencies with inner calm, the children responded in like manner. Where the parental response was highly emotionalized, the anxiety and fear experienced by the children were even greater. As Dr. Menninger has pointed out in *Love Against Hate*, the child, like a movie screen, reflects in greatly enlarged form the conflicts, tensions, and anxieties of his parents. The Biblical insight that "the parents have eaten sour grapes and the children's teeth are stood on edge" is sound psychological as well as moral observation. Acts of selfishness and words of prejudice seen and heard by the child are likely to be imitated. And on a deeper level, insecurity and fear—the very roots of selfishness and prejudice—are subtly transmitted from parent to child.

Certainly one of the objectives of introducing religion into the home—if not the ultimate objective—is the teaching of morality. But morality has deep roots in the psychic life of the individual and depends on the proper integration of his various motivations. If an individual is to be morally sound, his psyche must first be sound. The parent interested in the spiritual welfare of his children cannot rely on religious practices to work a miracle, transforming the raw stuff of human nature into angelic patterns. It is by cultivating religious attitudes that we can best create a religious atmosphere in the home and foster spiritual values.

Like learning to play the violin, this must be worked at. It will not come by itself, nor merely by the repetition of ritual acts and phrases. This does not gainsay the need for religious observance in the home. Rather, it points up the challenge to make of such religious observance not a substitute for but an instrument toward genuine spiritual growth.

The home is the earliest, strongest, and most enduring single influence in the life of an individual. It is here that values are transmitted and attitudes engendered. It is here that a way of life is not only taught but "caught," and built into the daily life of human beings. It is in the home that religious attitudes must be evidenced in all of the relations of all of its members.

Religion and Our Schools

What relationship is there, or ought there to be, between religion and our schools? This is a question that has evoked a good deal of discussion during the past decade, one which is still being widely debated. And it is, indeed, an important question.

As a people, we Americans have a high regard for education and seek to give our children as fine a schooling as possible. And we are, at least by our own assertions, a religious people, cherishing our religious freedom and the right of each man to go to the church of his choice. But we Americans, more than any other people (outside of the Communist countries), have erected a wall between religion and education. We have traditionally taken the attitude that, while religion and education are both desirable, they should be separated from each other.

But now there are those who, disturbed by the rise of juvenile delinquency and the state of private and public morality, and influenced by the present "return" to religion, feel that we may have gone too far in our separation of church and school. Religion, they feel, should be *a part of,* rather than *apart from,* education. They assert that the omission of religion in our public schools only makes the child think it is unimportant—less important than cooking or drawing. And, we are told, education deprived of religious coloration is not likely to produce the finest type of citizen, for a basic ingredient is missing from such education.

Men today are certainly better informed than they ever were. The ten-year-old boy knows more about electricity, geography, and many other subjects than did Socrates, Plato, or Isaiah. But does this mean that they are *better* men? Has private evil or public fraud diminished with the more widespread education of our day?

Some have lost faith in our public schools and have instead advocated and supported parochial schools sponsored by their religious denominations. Here, in addition to the material taught in the public schools, denominational religion is introduced as a part of the curriculum. This type of school has shown a remarkable growth during the past decade, a growth not restricted to one or even a few religious groups.

Others, however, do not go so far. They feel that we must not shun our public schools, that there is much that is valuable in them. But they feel that changes can be introduced *within* our schools: beginning the day with a prayer or a Bible reading, or releasing the child one afternoon a week somewhat earlier than usual so that he might go to his own church for religious instruction. Other suggestions have also been made, but these have been most commonly adopted.

While these procedures seem harmless enough, and are certainly preferable to the parochial school which would separate the children of America into creedal compartments, none of these plans is really compatible with our democratic heritage. For, if the parochial school represents an abandon-

ment and repudiation of the public school, these plans represent intrusions that run counter to the very *character* of our
public schools: the fact that they *are* secular, intentionally so.
Separated from direct religious influences, there emerged in
this country a new type of government and a new type of
school, the two most important bulwarks of our way of life.

The men who fashioned this nation sought to avoid
some of the difficulties and heartaches of the old world in the
building of the new. Religion has been in the past—and still
is, in many countries—closely connected with education.
The "democratic" West German government spends millions
of dollars annually for religious education in the schools, as
has long been the case in Germany. While religious education
in the schools should theoretically have made those peoples
exposed to it more just and humane, the facts have often been
otherwise. Indeed, religious differences have frequently become a source of friction within these nations.

But what is wrong with beginning each day at school
with a prayer or a Bible reading? Surely a prayer could be
found that would not be Christian, or Jewish, or Moham-
medan, but a *human* prayer? Or a Bible passage suitable to
all could be selected for reading before starting the day's
work. Yet even here there are difficulties: Who is to make the
selection? How is it to be presented? Much might depend on
the religious background of the teacher. Moreover, there
might be those in the class (or the teacher herself) who are
religiously unaffiliated, yet are taxed to support the schools.
Would such practices be fair to them?

But why object to the released-time plan for religious
education? The difficulty here lies in the fact that the public-
school bell, ringing to release the children for religious education, serves to separate them into different faith-groups.
They are no longer just American children at school but
Protestants, Catholics, Jews, *et al.* What of the child whose
parents are of a minority faith that has no church nearby,

or whose parents have no religious attachment? Might he not be marked as being somehow "different" from the rest?

Our schools are the symbol and seed-bed of democracy, in which all learn to live together as citizens of a democracy. The introduction of prayers or Bible readings, and even the released-time plan for religious education, may serve—and have already— as divisive factors in our schools, thus achieving the very opposite of what they were intended to achieve, building barriers instead of bridges between us. And is it not laziness, or a confession of failure on the part of the church, that it should want its work done by the schools?

To be sure, we do need the lessons of morality that religion can teach us—perhaps now more than ever. But religion itself is more than morality; it is also a body of belief, and beliefs differ. The religions of America have a more-or-less common morality; yet the morality of each is expressed through and colored by special beliefs and traditions. The churches and homes of America are best equipped to teach that morality, in the light of those beliefs and traditions. That is one of their primary functions.

They should not want to surrender that function to the public schools; indeed, they might only serve to weaken their own approaches to religion and morality. And the schools, on their part, should not want to accept that assignment, preferring, in keeping with the democratic tradition, that it be reserved for the church and the home, where the uniqueness of each of the faiths can be respected and preserved.

There is, to be sure, a kind of American religion, or religion of democracy, emerging in this nation of ours. It is rooted in the Constitution and Declaration of Independence, in the writings of Thomas Jefferson, Abraham Lincoln, and Walt Whitman. And it has been enriched by the moral insights and teachings of the various religious philosophies imported to these shores and indigenous to this nation.

Between the "religion of democracy" and the religions

of our democracy, there has been interaction. Democracy has had an impact on all of these religions, so that their institutions and approaches are not exactly the same here as they are in other countries. Each of these religions has probably had some impact on the other. And all, in their combined spiritual influence, have had a profound impact on our conception of democracy itself.

The "religion of democracy" is a fine distillation of the moral message of each of our religious traditions, expressed in terms of American ideals. The policy of "fair play" is an American rendition of the religion of the prophet Amos, who spoke of justice. The "good neighbor" policy is an American translation of religion's Golden Rule, common to Christianity, Judaism, and other great religions. This religion of democracy—this religion which *is* democracy—*belongs* in our schools. But sectarian religion does not.

The *religions* of our democracy can serve to strengthen the *religion* of democracy, and the religion of democracy can serve to express what is best in the religions of our democracy. Thus, the religion of democracy, taught by the schools, and the religions of our democracy, taught by church and home, can both contribute toward the building of a better America, stronger in its awareness and more consistent in its application of spiritual ideals.

The Color of One's Skin

In Sinclair Lewis' *Kingsblood Royal*, one of the characters remarks that there is no more difference between a white man and a black man than between a white cat and a black cat. Yet, interestingly enough, special feelings have attached themselves to the black cat, as they have come to be associated with the Negro. The matter of race, not only as regards the Negro, but the Oriental as well, has become a fertile field for the growth of many misconceptions.

One of the dominant myths of the western world is that of the superior white man. Yet this is but an indication of our own ethno-centrism, of our own "racial pride." Indeed, such superiority has been claimed by others besides the white man. There is a legend among the American Indians that when God set out to create man, he put some dough into the oven to bake. But He baked it too long, and out came the black man. Next He put another piece of dough into the oven, and this time, being a bit too careful, took it out too soon. As a result, we have the white man, the "pale-face." Finally, He took another piece of dough, put it into the oven, watched it very carefully, and it came out just right—the perfect man, the red man.

Religion long ago recognized that men do differ in the color of their skin, and long ago insisted that this should make no difference to us. The classic statement of this idea is to be found in the prophet Amos, speaking in the middle of the eighth century before the Christian era. He proclaimed, "Are ye not as the children of the Ethiopians unto Me, O children of Israel? Did I not bring up Israel out of the land of Egypt, and the Philistines from Caphtor, and the Syrians from Kir?" Speaking for God, Amos insists that the Hebrews are no better than the Ethiopians or Philistines or Syrians, that white man and black are alike in the sight of God.

The Bible tells us that all men are descended from a common ancestor, from Adam. Regardless of the theology involved, there is a striking implication in this idea: Let no man say his ancestry is better than another's. The Midrash, a collection of medieval homiletical material, tells a story of Alexander the Great and his Negro slave. The slave once walked into the palace with a burlap bag slung over his shoulders. Alexander, moved by curiosity, asked him what was in the sack. "Some human bones," replied the slave. Then Alexander asked, "Whose bones are they?," and the slave replied, "The bones of your ancestors and mine." Finally,

Alexander inquired, "But what are you doing with those bones?," and the slave replied, "I want to see if there is any difference between them." And the Midrash reports he found none.

The belief in the equality of the races finds expression in the literature of the great world religions. The concept of the Fatherhood of God involves as a corollary the Brotherhood of Man. But is this scientific? Or is it just an expression of "good will"?

It is more than that. The best of scientific research serves to support the insights of religion in this matter. The late Franz Boas, the anthropologist who taught at Columbia University for many years, came to the conclusion that while there are backward and advanced races—races that have gone further than others—there are no inferior and superior races. The distinction is tremendously significant. It indicates that there is nothing inherent in the groups of mankind to make them advanced or backward, that their status is the result of circumstance rather than genetics.

Religious insight long ago postulated the essential equality of the races of mankind. Men in our day, who have had the benefit of scientific investigation confirming that insight, should be ready to recognize it. They have nonetheless flouted it, have refused to accept it—not only in South Africa, but in our country as well. The Nazi movement in Germany developed its own theories of race, asserting that there were not only physical differences between Nordics and non-Nordics but also mental and spiritual differences, adding insult to injury and fantasy to fiction.

H. G. Wells, in one of his stories, tells of the man who had heard that "in the land of the blind, the one-eyed man is king." He learned of the location of the land of the blind and undertook the long and difficult journey to that country in the hope that he, a one-eyed man, might rule over them. But he was received with a great deal of suspicion. He was not allowed to mingle freely with them, to eat with them, or engage in social intercourse with them. After all, he was "different."

So it is with the matter of race. Where racial egotism is involved, and the latent, primitive fear of the stranger—to say nothing of economic motivations and social habits of behavior—the color of one's skin becomes a barrier to brotherhood. And so, ironically enough, it is difficult to implement in practice the religious concept of human equality even within the church. The decision of the Supreme Court calling for the racial integration of the public schools has served to remind the more sensitive members of the churches of America that "eleven o'clock Sunday morning is the most segregated hour in American life." One could perhaps observe that in a field where the religious forces of America should have led, they are now compelled to follow. Yet that would not be altogether fair. For we can hardly estimate the extent to which the teachings of religion have influenced the increasing acceptance of racial equality in America, influenced even the members of the Supreme Court of this land.

But the opportunities and responsibilities of religious leaders do not rest there. The social and psychological roots of prejudice must be examined and discussed so that more churchgoers may be made capable of loving their neighbors as themselves. Now that scientific evidence serves to support time-honored religious contentions that all men are equal; now that the very laws of our land move forward to see that they are treated as equals; and now that more men are turning to the institutions of religion for guidance in their lives, the representatives of religion must meet the challenge of preparing men spiritually for new horizons in race relations and leading them toward their attainment.

The Problem of Peace

During the Civil War, Abraham Lincoln was asked whether he thought God was on his side. He replied that what bothered him was not whether God was on *his* side, but whether *he* was on *God's*.

Lincoln recognized that ethical rightness is not determined by might; that the act of war is a refutation of religion's most basic precepts. Religion teaches, "Thou shalt not kill," insisting on the sacredness of human life; war is a negation of that principle, for men are "expendable" in the achievement of a military objective. Religion teaches the brotherhood of man; war is a denial of human brotherhood, for brothers do not—or should not—slay one another. Religion asks that men be governed by the law of morality; war is governed by the law of expediency: any step will be taken, any weapon will be used, if it will lead to military victory.

Indeed, from the viewpoint of religion, resort to war is based on several questionable assumptions.

The first of these is that "our side" is right and the "other side" wrong. Our thinking in war is somewhat like that exhibited in wild west movies, where the villain is painted very black indeed, and the hero lily-white. (It has even been observed that the hero in these movies generally wears a light-colored hat, the villain a black one, to help dramatize the distinction!) But in real life this is rarely so, or judges would have an easy time in trying the cases that come before them. Instead, they are required to use their best knowledge and finest judgment in determining at what point in the claims of two litigants justice and truth are really to be found.

In international relations, infinitely more complex than interpersonal ones, it is even harder to determine who is "right" and who is "wrong." To label the other side "wrong," as one does in going to war, is to see the mote in the eye of the other without seeing the beam in our own. "Judge not,

that ye be not judged" is as important in international as in
interpersonal affairs. Religious morality would oppose ascribing guilt and casting blame; it would oppose the pride of self-
righteousness thus displayed.

Yet even allowing for the possibility that the "other
side" may be wrong, or more wrong than we are, there is a
second questionable assumption involved in resort to war:
that our side had little or nothing to do with *making* the other
side wrong. This is highly improbable. War may "break out"
suddenly, yet it is likely to be preceded by a whole history of
antecedent acts and attitudes. Was the First World War
"caused" by the assassination of the Archduke of Austria at
Sarajevo? Forty years ago we may have thought so; not today.

The steps that lead to war are rarely reviewed before
going to war; they become subject-matter for historians *after*
the war. And the accounts are usually colored by the historians' own national loyalties. If the fabled man from Mars
were to write a history of the wars of mankind from his ideal
vantage-point and with his presumed objectivity, it would
probably read differently from the accounts of their origins
written thus far.

In interpersonal relations, we generally find that people
treat us pretty much as we treat them. There is a kind of
"reciprocity" between us. Is there not a similar reciprocity in
international relations? If, as individuals, we are disliked by
other individuals, we should ask ourselves not only what is
wrong with them, but also what is wrong with us. And if, as a
nation, we are at loggerheads with other nations, the same
thing ought to be true. We need not decide that those on the
other side are *right*, but we may discover that we have helped
to make them *wrong*.

But suppose that we find the other side to be wrong,
and find further that we had nothing to do with bringing
that about. (This is theoretically conceivable, although we
would have difficulty finding an example.) If one goes to

war at this point, one makes another questionable assumption: that war alone will settle the problem. There may still be untried peaceful alternatives; and war does not really settle any problems. These have to be solved at the conference table after the war—by the same men and nations who have shown their inability to settle them without resort to war! In addition, war itself produces a host of new problems—economic dislocation, displaced populations, etc.—and creates feelings of resentment and revenge on the part of the vanquished nation, so that the "victory" hardly "pays."

Now that war has been rendered more destructive than ever, we are compelled to think about it more basically than before. We know that war is a method of solving, or attempting to solve, international tensions. It is not a part of "human nature," any more than duelling once was, or "shooting it out" in the days of the frontier. Men still quarrel, but our courts, backed by police power, now adjudicate those quarrels.

We in America can perhaps best discern the pattern required for a world at peace. We have integrated fifty states into one nation. This integration has been three-fold: political, economic, and psychological or spiritual. Does not this suggest the pattern to be followed if we want to have peace, if we want "one world"? Must we not think in terms of increasing political, economic, and spiritual integration of the peoples of the earth? As the international political agency for peace, the United Nations must be given more specific discretion and power to preserve peace. On the economic level, barriers to trade among the nations must be reduced, and the still backward nations must be helped to help themselves make the most of their own resources. On the spiritual front, world-mindedness must be cultivated; we must see that we are all part of the same human family, that we must all learn to live together harmoniously.

It is on the last of these fronts that religion can best

serve. Nor is this the least important part of the tasks ahead, for the creation of world-mindedness, the feeling of world brotherhood, is essential if the first two objectives are to be consistently pursued. The conviction that all mankind is one must be the conviction underlying all of our efforts to eliminate war.

Shortly after the close of World War II, I saw a display of objects taken from the enemy dead. There were the customary helmets, swords, and guns. There was also a German Bible, pierced by a bullet-hole and stained with blood. That Bible, carried over the heart of some German lad, did not save that youth's life. It served only to sanctify slaughter, his death and the death of those he slew. As I looked at that Bible, I thought of boys who might have used Bibles in English, in French, and in other languages, in much the same manner, yet whose lives were not spared. A tragic irony lies in the fact that in this book were not only words which could aid men to face the hazards of war, but also those which could inspire men to eliminate war, to save that boy—and all young men, forever—from such cruel and unnecessary death.

How long must we wait? How long must we fail to implement its teachings? We have conquered the air and the oceans, have annihilated time and space, yet in the field of human relationships and in the relationships between nation and nation we have made little advance out of the jungle. Indeed, the jungle has never known the carnage that took place at Hiroshima. We have yet to learn the meaning of human brotherhood. We have yet to learn to shed suspicion and fear and hate, to practice sincerity and faith in our dealings with others. This is what our past patterns of diplomacy have all too often demonstrated.

But the responsibility is not alone the diplomats'. They represent to a marked degree their nations: they are a product of them, reflecting the narrowness or breadth of their nations' thinking. Not only they, but we, more urgently, must learn to think internationally. The spiritual insights of religion must be rendered vital in our behavior as individuals and as nations. The insights and moral teachings of religion are sound; they are, in spite of cynicism and doubt, practical. They will work, if given half a chance. Through their application, and only through their application, will we be able to create "new men, new nations, and a new world."

Unfinished Business

It has been suggested that the Biblical phrase, "In the *beginning* God created . . . ," implies that God left a good deal for man to do in completing the work of creation.

As we think of the contemporary scene, we find many areas in which ethical religion can and ought to give us guidance in shaping our attitudes and actions. Some of these issues are not as frequently discussed as the problems of race relations and peace. Yet they, too, are important, involving moral considerations that cannot permanently be side-stepped.

One of these issues is capital punishment. This is one of the lingering barbarities of the twentieth century—or will be so regarded in centuries to come. And it is a bit surprising that the forces of religion, concerned with the large issues of peace and race relations, have not been equally concerned with this problem.

The question is raised in our minds, however, when we read that England has recently debated the matter in Parliament. It pops up again as we discover in a newspaper filler that several foreign countries do not practice capital punishment except for treason. Or it comes up for discussion after a good dinner, when one of the dinner guests may feel more benevolent than usual and provoke a discussion of it by referring to it as immoral.

We have sought to render capital punishment—like

war—"humane," avoiding too much pain to the person and too much damage to the body. Perhaps of the two, more concern has been shown for injury to the body, or the guillotine, certainly a swift form of death, might be more universally employed. (Indeed, since "capital punishment" means punishment by removal of the head, we should probably reinstate the guillotine, or change the term!)

Through the effort to render capital punishment more "humane," we have tried to mitigate its immorality. But it may well be that rendering the action more "humane" only serves to perpetuate it. If we still stoned or flogged men to death, the immorality of the action might be more apparent and capital punishment the sooner eliminated.

We may well speculate why capital punishment has survived to this day in so large a part of the "civilized" world. On a psychoanalytic level, it has been suggested that we slay the murderer because we envy him. We have all at one time or another wanted to do what he did, but dared not. Now we can do it—to him—without fear of the consequences, and with even a sense of our own superiority and self-righteousness.

How valid this explanation is, I will not attempt to assess. Yet it is striking that every "reason" advanced for the use of capital punishment is not very convincing. That it prevents further instances of criminality by others is highly doubtful. That it serves to eliminate the offender is true— but there are other ways to put him out of circulation. One cannot escape the conclusion that capital punishment is just that—an expression of our own punitive urge.

We now know enough about sociology and psychology to recognize that environmental influences and internal conflicts have contributed to a criminal's career. Dr. Robert Lindner, in *The Fifty-Minute Hour*, has provided some fascinating insights into the twisted minds and souls of prisoners, which can but give us pause before the urge to punish.

We have already reached that stage in the practice of law where we recognize the existence of the "criminally insane" individual and treat him somewhat specially. We must someday recognize that no criminal is truly "sane" and do something more than destroy him. If psychiatry seeks to understand the criminal rather than to punish him, the forces of religion, morally oriented toward an acceptance of the importance of the individual—yes, even in the case of the criminal—must do no less.

Religious considerations are also involved in another issue, one which has recently received considerable discussion—euthanasia, or mercy killing. There have been several cases in the past ten years in which doctors and others have been put on trial for such killings. Indeed, the attempt to make euthanasia legal is actually being promoted by agencies devoted to that purpose. It is an idea to which some people of learning and good character have responded; an idea which seems to appeal to our humanitarian and religious impulses. For it is certainly anguishing to stand by the bed of a loved one dying slowly and painfully, and the urge to help him is strong—even to the point of ending his suffering with death.

It may be that those who speak for euthanasia are perfectly moral persons, perhaps nobler and more compassionate toward the suffering than ourselves. We may indeed be blinding ourselves to the possibility that death may sometimes *be* the lesser of two evils and lack the moral courage to champion euthanasia. Yet there is the inevitable suspicion that the mercy-killer, though consciously acting on noble impulse, may be revealing—or concealing—through that action subconscious urges to kill and destroy that are latent in us all. I will not push this point, and may even be mistaken, yet the haunting doubt, based on our psychiatric insights into the subtle workings of the subconscious, ought at least to be expressed.

Aside from this approach to the problem, there are

moral and religious considerations here involved that cry out
for clarification. That the mercy-killer himself may presumably be prompted by such considerations does not lessen but
increases the need to clarify the issue. We must know *why*
we oppose euthanasia if we are to offset the appeal of this
idea to some of our most thoughtful people. We must be able
to meet them on their own moral ground and convince them
on the spiritual and religious level that euthanasia is wrong.

We need not go into the mechanics of mercy-killing:
that it would be done only upon the request of the patient
or his family, with the advice and consent of the attending
physician and with court permission. All this should be taken
for granted if mercy-killing is not to become simple murder.
The problem lies deeper than all this.

Human society is a strange thing. Extremes often meet.
Primitive societies often practice polygamy. Yet the sophis-
ticates of Hollywood also practice polygamy; sequential,
rather than static polygamy—they never have more than one
wife at a time. So too with the matter of mercy-killing. Primitive groups have been known to kill their sick, their aged,
and even defective children, so that euthanasia is really nothing new. Yet the most advanced segments of our society are
now taken with this idea.

Is the euthanasia practiced by more primitive groups,
then, a high level of moral behavior? Should we now emulate
it, adding only the improved techniques of science and the
safeguards of law? We have lately begun to appreciate the
uses of reserpine and other herbal medications used long ago
by less advanced peoples, for the treatment of mental illness.
Is the ancient or more primitive practice of mercy-killing
perhaps morally sound after all?

Not so long as reverence for life is a dominating concept
in our religious thinking. Not so long as science keeps discovering new ways to put an end to disease or new ways to
make its ravages less painful. What may have been morally

defensible once is no longer as defensible. But there is an even more basic consideration. Once human beings arrogate to themselves the right to decide who shall live and who shall die, the flood-gates of man's demonic urges may be opened, his deepest diabolical drives be unleashed. Witness the systematic extermination of the Jews in Nazi Germany. Why not then proceed to destroy the "unfit," the handicapped, the blind, the deaf, and the mute? This too has been done by more primitive peoples. Yet such practices on our part would have robbed us of Helen Keller and other "unfit" persons who achieved greatness.

The Talmud, an encyclopedic commentary on Biblical law, observes that we must not touch the bed of a dying person, lest death be hastened to the slightest degree. There is profundity and sublimity in that statement. Preserving and enriching life is the highest expression of religious morality. Destroying or degrading life is the essence of irreligion and immorality, whatever the expressed motives may be. The deed cannot be justified: the end does not justify the means, even where the elimination of suffering is the presumed goal.

History is too full of the record of men burned at the stake to save their souls for us to fall prey to such reasoning. Science is too full of the promise of prevention and the prospect of cure; psychiatry has made us too aware of the subconscious element in much of our thought and behavior; and religious morality is too convinced of the sacredness of life, too humble before God's handiwork, to permit us to resort to mercy-killing.

Just one more entry in our Unfinished Business—though others could be added. This is the matter of birth control, or, as it should be more properly known, planned parenthood. Here is a movement which has grown slowly but steadily in public acceptance, and has been increasingly endorsed by our religious groups. Yet because it still meets with opposition in some quarters on religious grounds, because its victory is not yet fully won, and because it involves the religious principles of reverence for life and human personality, it ought to be mentioned.

While the case for planned parenthood by now needs little defending, it does require understanding. For it is possible that something may be approved and espoused, yet for the wrong reasons. I have no doubt that many who approve and practice the spacing of children or family limitation do so for selfish reasons: they may be seeking, consciously or unconsciously, to reduce or avoid the inconveniences and responsibilities involved in raising a family. Yet that does not negate the basic morality of the movement itself.

We plan a trip, the purchase of a home or a car. Should we not also plan our family—something infinitely more precious and meaningful? Should we not see to it that our children are wanted, not foisted upon us? We now know the psychological impact of the unwanted child upon parents, and the degree to which that impact may be transmitted to the child himself. Should we not "space" the family so that each child can receive the proper attention, affection and education?

Considerations of the health of the mother, her exposure to possible danger in childbirth, her limitations of strength to care for the child after birth, are also important. These too are moral considerations, sufficient to justify the practice of planned parenthood.

Conversely—for family planning works both ways— should we not try to overcome the blight of barrenness, to determine its causes and develop cures, to bring added joy and meaning into the lives of childless couples, or to provide an only child with the companionship of brothers or sisters for his healthy emotional growth?

There is no disregard for the sanctity of life involved in planned parenthood, no attempt to take life, only a desire to make life better for parent and child. And this is, or should be, a religious objective.

There is indeed unfinished business left for the adherent
of mature religion, in these and in other areas of contemporary living—the displacement of labor by increasing automa-
tion, our responsibility to the aged as life is prolonged, etc.
Motivated by a reverential regard for human life and personality, and fully informed—knowing what we are about—we
can make our faith more than a refuge from the problems of
life. We can make of it an arsenal of the spirit, to strengthen
us in the struggle for their ultimate conquest.

The World We Want to Live In

Once man lived in the dark ages of scarcity, when life
was necessarily hard, and all of his work was done with his
own hands and his own back. In that pioneering period he
had at his disposal only the most rudimentary tools: the
wheel, the inclined plane, the lever. The shoes he wore, the
clothes on his body, the house he lived in, were made by
hand, consuming much time and energy.

During those times, too, the means of travel and communication were limited. The interchange of goods, as well as
ideas, was slow. If drought occurred in one section of the
country, it was weeks before the news spread, and people in
the affected area perished before help could arrive. If a useful
discovery was made in one area, it took many months before
others heard of it and could benefit by it.

With the advent of the industrial revolution, mechanical
power replaced human labor. Engineering replaced pioneering. Mass production enabled many to have the things that
few had possessed before. Other great changes took place.
New methods of communication and transport made the
world smaller and made for the speedy exchange of ideas and
goods, also making each man dependent on others, hundreds
or even thousands of miles away, for the things he used. The
use of coal, of oil, and of water-power produced a world of

more goods, speedier communication, and greater interdependence than ever before.

But these developments brought problems in their wake. The industrial revolution produced new and expanding nationalisms, new national arts and cultures, but also led to enslaving colonialism. Material progress produced greater wealth, but also the sweat shop. Speedy transportation produced more trade, but greater competition in the world's markets. Rapid communication produced greater enlightenment, but also the spread of propaganda. Mass production produced the automobile, but also the bombing plane. Scientific research produced medical cures, but also intercontinental missiles. A more highly interdependent world produced international agencies of peace, health and education, but also far-reaching military alliances.

At this point, our generation stands—and a new challenge confronts us. Just as the age of scarcity was followed by the age of engineering, so must the age of engineering— which has already become the space age—lead to an age of humanizing. The next forward step must consist in the application of the power and the knowledge we possess to the solution of our human and social problems.

Some time ago I saw an exhibit which perhaps points up the challenge. In a glass case were all of the raw materials that went into the making of an automobile. There were a few pounds of steel, a few sheets of rubber, some zinc, tin, nails, screws, and upholstery cloth. This, the inscription on the glass case said, represented all the materials constituting one automobile.

Yet all of these materials would not in themselves make an automobile. Mixed together in a giant mortar, they could not produce an operating mechanism. Something else was necessary—human ingenuity, human imagination, activated by the desire to *have* an automobile.

Samuel Butler once wrote a book entitled *Erewhon,* in

which he presented a Utopia, an ideal society. The fictional visitor to Erewhon is shown through that country and is impressed with what he sees: schools, hospitals, homes. Then he is taken to a museum, where he is shown some fabulous machinery: steam-engines, airships, and labor-saving devices of all kinds. He remarks to his host how strange it seems that the country, having made such advances, does not make use of them but relegates them to a museum instead. His host replies that these had once been put to use but they produced many problems, so they were abandoned.

It is quite some time since Butler wrote that novel, in which he anticipated some of the difficulties of our day. It was ironic indeed that the very men who invented these devices had not the ingenuity to render them a blessing rather than a burden. And it would be equally ironic if we, who are the heirs to the industrial revolution, could not work through the problems it has engendered, to achieve the promise it still holds forth.

Our civilization is indeed complex. And it has been suggested that modern man is "obsolete," unable to cope with its problems, just as the dinosaur could not cope with the coming of the ice age and disappeared. Yet we know that man's adaptive mechanism is far more subtle and far more able than the dinosaur's to aid in his adjustment. For the adaptive mechanism of man is not external—he does not have to grow more hair, or a new hide, to protect him against the elements—but internal. It lies within him.

Many, many centuries ago, man learned to stand upright. He learned to make clubs and spears, then the wheel. The first revolution of the first wheel made a great revolution in his capacities and considerably altered his habits. He has been "making wheels" ever since, both literally and figuratively, producing new revolutions in his habits of thought and conduct.

We stand now on the verge of another such revolution—

a moral revolution, engendered by the absurdity of poverty in an age of abundance, the stupidity of prejudice in an age of increasing literacy, the brutality of war in an age of power. Now that we have entered upon the ultimate phase of the age of engineering—the space age—the urgency of that moral revolution is made more manifest. We possess not only the material requirements but also the needed spiritual resources. And we are bound to harness their strength. For man, akin to nature, which he seeks increasingly to understand, is also akin to God, striving to express the divinity within him.

Here lies much of the paradox of life, its restless tension. Man struggles to subdue the beast in him and express the best in him—the beauty and goodness that are part of his endowment. He falters and falls, and even fails, yet "divine discontent" drives him onward to new successes and new achievements in the realm of the spirit. He is inspired by the conviction that love is worth while, though it meet with rebuff; that effort is meaningful, though it meet with failure. He moves forward, or is carried forward, by a force within himself, yet greater than himself, in the attempt to convert ugliness into beauty, chaos into order—to convert the raw materials of life into a mansion of the soul.

CHAIN REACTION

By now we are all somewhat familiar with the process by which atomic power is released—the chain reaction. It is the action of particle upon particle, atom upon atom, that produces the effect.

What happens is comparable to what takes place in a game of billiards. When one billiard ball is hit, it will strike others in turn. The force and angle of the cue stick's impact on the first ball will determine the speed, direction, and distance travelled by that ball and all the others. And within that "chain reaction" each of the balls affects the ball it strikes in like manner. The billiard balls display an interlocking interaction.

But "chain reaction" is not restricted to the release of atomic power or to the movement of billiard balls. There is chain reaction—interaction—on a universal scale. There is cause and effect in all of the phenomena of nature. And the cause and effect are commensurate with each other. "Every action has an equal and opposite reaction" is one way of putting it. In the realm of light transmission, "the angle of incidence is equal to the angle of reflection." The effect is invariably related to the cause; its magnitude is conditioned by that cause.

There is constant interaction in nature, even where no action is involved. In Einstein's field theory—at least as the layman understands it—there is not only a magnetic *force* between objects, but a magnetic *field* as well. Though stationary, they are invisibly affecting each other, affecting the very space between them. No two objects are totally detached from one another, completely "indifferent" to one another. They are constantly "influencing" each other.

What is true in the realm of nature is true of human nature; what is true in the realm of physics is equally true in the realm of ethics—in all of our human relationships. There is constant interaction between ourselves and those around us. The things we do, the things we say, have an influence on others commensurate with the character of that deed or word. Indeed, following the analogy of the "field," what we are and what we think, the way we feel and the very attitudes we harbor, affect others—affect the very space between us.

The religious formulation of this law of human interaction is expressed in the statement, "As ye sow, so shall ye reap." In the relationships between men, as in nature, we cannot plant cabbages and reap tomatoes. We cannot plant suspicion and breed trust, we cannot plant hate and breed love. There is a kind of retribution here involved. The good we do is likely to be returned to us, or at the least sent out into the world to make it better. And the evil that we do is fraught with similar consequences. This is true in our individual relationships; it is equally true on the level of international relations. It is part of the interlocking, interacting dynamics of life.

Much that we see in the world about us is disheartening and depressing. There is so much selfishness and immorality, corruption and deceit that we can easily be discouraged from acting differently. What can our own attitudes, our own efforts, really amount to? Yet we know that chain reactions can be produced; that there is within us moral power which can be released—power enough, in chain reaction, to produce a spiritual explosion.

Men have started such chain reactions throughout history. And men are still starting them. Consider the case of Raphael Lemkin. His is the saga of one man's determination to eradicate a terrible crime. He gave that crime a name—genocide, the mass murder of members of a single ethnic or religious group. And he devoted his time, his energy, his whole being, to making genocide recognized as a crime—as it now is—in the councils of nations. He was only one man. But Moses was only one man; and so was Confucius, and Jesus, and Gandhi. And what far-reaching chain reactions they set in motion!

The story is told of a woman living in a small town in West Virginia who wanted very much to be invited to become a member of the local woman's club but was never invited to join. She began to feel that this was because she might be too dull and uninteresting a person. She decided to make a trip to Europe, to broaden her experiences. Shortly after she got there, however, bombs began to fall all around her—World War II broke out. Having some training as a nurse, she offered her services in treating the injured and "worked out" the war in that fashion. Upon her return home, she completely forgot her previous ambition. And when someone asked her what she had been doing in Europe, she simply replied, "Holding back hell."

Each of us can make some contribution to that effort. Each of us can do his share, however small it may seem, to reduce the amount of fear and hate, insecurity and insincerity we find around us, by what we say and do, by what we are. We need not try to transform the world, if we can but transform our community. We need not even try to transform our community, if we but transform ourselves. For each of us born into this world is like a stone cast into a pool of water: the waves we produce go on and on and affect a wider orbit than we know.